D1075167

Preaching

BY LESLIE J. TIZARD

Guide to Marriage

LESLIE J. TIZARD

Preaching
The Art of Communication

In preaching there is intended a communion
of souls, and a communication of somewhat
from ours unto theirs.
> Richard Baxter, *The Reformed Pastor*
> Chapter 5

FOREWORD BY
DR LESLIE E. COOKE

OXFORD UNIVERSITY PRESS   NEW YORK   1959

Printed in the United States of America

CONTENTS

FOREWORD

THIS foreword is written in response to the request of a dying man who knew that he was dying. In one of his last letters to me in which he told me of the doctor's diagnosis of his illness, Leslie Tizard spoke about this book on preaching which he was hastening to complete. He recalled that we had often talked together about preaching and that he had informed his publishers that he was sure that I would write a foreword to this book and indeed complete it if he had to leave it unfinished. I suspect that he would have written more than is contained in these chapters and amplified and polished what he had already written had there been time.

These chapters which he has given to us are in fact based upon a series of lectures which he was preparing against the day when a suggestion to deliver a well-known American series of lectures on preaching would mature into an official invitation. He was looking forward to this possibility and therefore withheld publishing anything on this subject lest he be guilty of a discourtesy or an injustice to those who were responsible for the lectureship. It was when he knew that he would never be able to accept such an invitation that he began to put his material in order for this book. The book reveals that Leslie Tizard had theological students and young preachers especially in mind when he was writing. He was anxious to share with them not only his experiences as a preacher but his own high conception of the preacher's calling so that his readers would be inspired as well as technically helped as they prepared themselves for their task.

Those who are acquainted with the long series of books on preaching will be familiar with much of the ground which the author of this book covers, but they will find here evidence of that same gift of lucid interpretation which characterised all Mr Tizard's speaking and writing and a convincing apologia for the preacher's calling in an age of highly developed techniques of communication.

Mr Tizard's own well-stored and cultured mind is reflected in these pages, so also is his own skill in the use of illustration as well as his own consecration to the preaching ministry. I suspect that his conse-cration was all the more complete because of an early experience when he had to pass through an inner struggle occasioned by an opportunity offered him when he was a young pastor of leaving the pulpit for a career in social service. These pages show, too, and some will value them most of all for this reason, the sympathy and imaginative under-standing of men and women which derived not only from the author's love for them but from his own continuous and honest self-examination in the sight of God and his own acknowledged dependence on God's Grace.

Had Mr Tizard lived, I venture to believe that he would have done fuller justice in this book to a dimension of his preaching which those who knew him and heard him always sensed: his insight into the Gospel he proclaimed which had its source in his own personal de-votion to Christ. I recall particularly his London Missionary Society sermon preached to the Assembly of the Congregational Union of England and Wales in Westminster Chapel, and his sermon preached to the Free Church Congress in Northampton as particular examples of these qualities of his preaching. On the other hand, perhaps only his living personality in the pulpit could have adequately revealed these qualities, and they must remain the cherished and precious memories of those who knew and heard him. To readers who had the privilege of sitting under Mr Tizard, this book will recall experiences when they knew what it means to speak of 'the sacrament of the Word of God'. To those who never heard him this book will ennoble their conception of the preacher's task. For all of us this book is in very truth the word of 'a dying man to dying men', which all preaching ought to be, and which for Mr Tizard it always was.

LESLIE E. COOKE

Geneva April 23rd 1958

CHAPTER ONE

What Preaching Is

As a student I had a distinction which I can speak of freely since it was in no sense an achievement of mine, but due solely to chance. I was, I believe, the last student interviewed for admission to college by Principal Peter Taylor Forsyth. As I look back over the years, that experience remains something of a nightmare. I was a callow youth of seventeen. I had never read a word of his theology and should not have understood it if I had tried, but it had been impressed upon me by my minister that Forsyth was a great man—a very great man. That was why I was to seek entrance to his college. I was shown into his study—a rather grim and forbidding room as I recall it. At last Forsyth entered. He was ill and ageing. I remember his pale face and his beard, his slippers and his velvet coat. I felt still more that the whole thing was a mistake. The interview did not go well. Forsyth was then a little hard of hearing and his voice had become rather feeble, so that I sometimes could not be sure I had caught his words. I was saved, I think, by his colleague and son-in-law, Professor H. T. Andrews, who acted as an intermediary. He seemed somehow to know what I had tried to say in my halting replies, or what I ought to have said! Suddenly Forsyth asked: 'If you had only one sermon to preach, what would you preach about?' I looked appealingly at Andrews, to whom I was devoted from that day until his all-too-early death, but even he could not make bricks in the entire absence of straw. At last Forsyth himself broke the silence. 'Well,' he asked, 'can you tell us what was the text of your *first* sermon?' That was easy, for I had only two, or at the most three. 'It was', I replied eagerly, ' "By the grace of

God I am what I am".' The great man looked pleased, and I felt that things had taken a turn for the better. 'A wonderful text!' he said, 'A wonderful text!'

Yes, a wonderful text, though I shudder to think of the sermon. Yet I believe I did try to preach. My dictionary tells me that to preach means 'to cry in public' or 'to proclaim by public discourse'. It makes no difference that my public numbered only some half-dozen patient souls gathered in a little country chapel on a hot Sunday morning. And I am sure I proclaimed with all the confidence of a boy of sixteen, nothing daunted by the fact that some of his hearers were old when he was born.

Let us pause a moment on the word 'proclaim', for it is the very heart of preaching. All true preaching is proclamation, although, of course, not all proclamation is preaching. You may proclaim anything, but you are not preaching in the Christian sense unless you are proclaiming what God is and what He has done.

Dr C. H. Dodd, in *The Apostolic Preaching and Its Developments*, has pointed out that 'The New Testament writers draw a clear distinction between preaching (*kerygma*) and teaching (*didache*). Teaching is, in a large majority of cases, ethical instruction. Preaching, on the other hand, is the public proclamation of Christianity to the non-Christian world. For the early Church, then, to preach the Gospel was by no means the same thing as to deliver moral exhortation. It was by *kerygma*, says Paul, not by *didache*, that it pleased God to save men.'

Preaching, then, is not primarily instruction. It is not argument. A sermon may, of course, contain argument. We may, and should, build up systematic arguments to convince the minds of our hearers. Paul certainly did that, and he employed the kind of argument most likely to carry weight with the congregation of the moment. And the sermon may also include moral instruction or exhortation arising from the truth which has been proclaimed. It may, indeed, offer a great deal that is profitable in all kinds of ways, but if it does not contain proclamation it is not preaching.

And it must be the proclamation of the Gospel, the good news of what God has done, is doing and will do.

Now this proclamation is threefold:

(1) We are to proclaim the historical facts through which God revealed Himself and acted for man's salvation. These facts are the birth, life, cross and resurrection of Jesus. 'God was in Christ reconciling the world unto himself.'

The Gospel which Paul believed himself called to preach was not a story which he had invented. It was a Gospel that had been entrusted to him by God. 'But as we were allowed of God to be put in trust with the Gospel, even so we speak' (I *Thessalonians* ii. 4). That Gospel he had received. It had been handed on to him in the Christian tradition by those who themselves had first-hand knowledge of the facts. 'For I delivered unto you first of all that which I also received, how that Christ died for our sins according to the scriptures; And that he was buried, and that he rose again the third day according to the scriptures . . .' (I *Corinthians* xv. 2 f.). In the same letter (xi. 23 ff.) he prefaces his account of the institution of the Lord's Supper with the words, 'For I have received of the Lord that which also I delivered unto you. . . .' He is not referring to any supernatural revelation by voice or vision. He is assuring his readers that those facts which he had communicated to them had come to him on the authority of those who were present that night and themselves saw the actions which Jesus did and heard the words which He spoke.

The Gospel is thus firmly rooted in history. We have no right to add to it or subtract from it. That great Congregationalist, Bernard Manning, of Cambridge, said: 'When our forefathers spoke of themselves as peculiarly free and owing their freedom to the Bible, they were thinking of the manifold burden of tradition and accretion that had gathered about the Faith since Apostolic times. They were thinking of the authority which Holy Scripture gave them for supposing that the Gospel of Christ did not depend on the inventions and appliances of a later age, useful as these might have been in their time.' Our Gospel is 'the faith once delivered to the saints' (*Jude* 3), delivered to Paul, delivered to every true preacher since, and it is ours to proclaim it.

(2) We are to proclaim what God has done through Christ in human experience. 'By the grace of God I am what I am.' When Forsyth said it was a wonderful text I think he meant that it is one which takes a preacher to the heart of the Gospel. No preacher, unless he be a man of singular ingenuity, can announce that text and then waste his time on trivialities and topicalities. He has committed himself to tell what God can do in and through a human life. I hope you will believe that when I preached on that text at the age of sixteen I did not hold myself up as a trophy of God's grace but that I tried to set forth Paul as the proof of His saving and transforming power. That should have been enough to occupy me in what was, I believe, a shorter sermon than I now commonly inflict on my hearers. I think the mature preacher should go farther. He must proclaim the grace of God from his own experience and observation. He has seen what God can do in the twentieth century as well as in the first, whether it be in the plucking of a brand from the burning, or in 'a difficult temperament overcome' in which, says Professor J. A. Findlay, Paul found the chief evidence of God's effectual working within himself. Above all, the mature preacher must speak with a conviction born of the knowledge that God has been at work in his own soul. 'Beware', said Richard Baxter, 'lest you be void of the saving grace that you offer to others.'

(3) We must proclaim that what God has done for others and for ourselves He can do, and will do, for any man. There is no 'good news' in the affirmation that God's saving power was given to men centuries ago, or to me yesterday, unless I can assure the most needy hearer that it will be given to him today. There is no Gospel in condemnation nor in confronting a man with moral demands to which he knows that he will never be able to respond in his own strength. The Gospel is the good news of God's promises made freely and unconditionally to any

man who will receive them in simple trust—promises that are utterly reliable. 'No one who puts his trust in Him will ever be disappointed. No one.'

It is clear that when we are really preaching we are not merely making a speech or 'giving an address'. We are speaking on behalf of God as though God were entreating by us. We can go further. Preaching is not the activity of man alone; it is not merely a man who is speaking. God is speaking through him. In other words, the preacher when he is really preaching, which is not always, is an inspired man. But the word 'inspiration' is used with such a wide range of meanings that we had better try to see in what sense we are using it here.

The idea that a man might be inspired is, of course, a very old one. In its more primitive forms inspiration is thought to be complete possession by the god to the exclusion of all conscious processes. When the god is in the man is out. This god-possession is described as a 'divine seizure' or a 'brief madness', which does not mean insanity but the complete control of the mental faculties by a supernatural power. Such ideas of inspiration still obtain in Tibet and elsewhere. In the Old Testament, on the lower spiritual levels inspiration is sometimes of this kind. There were 'schools of the prophets' who cultivated religious frenzies and ecstasies which apparently could be infectious, for we are told that three relays of messengers sent by Saul to bring home David all succumbed 'when they saw the company of the prophets prophesying', and Saul himself eventually proved to be just as susceptible. The New Testament 'gift of tongues' is possession of the same kind. It is supposed that the Spirit takes control of all the mental faculties of the worshipper and speaks through him in his state of ecstasy in which he is oblivious of his surroundings. No specimen of the speaking with tongues in New Testament times has come down to us, but Monsignor Ronald Knox, in his great work on *Enthusiasm*, quotes examples from the church of Edward Irving which, he says, are beyond the reach of any lexicon. 'Such utterances as "Hippo gerosto niparos boorastin farini O fastor sungor boorinos epongos menati", or "Hey amei hassan alla do hoc alora iloore has heo massan amor ho ti prov his aso me", hardly bear out the claim that "the languages are distinct, well-inflected, well-compacted languages". The philology of another world does not abide our question, but if we are to judge these results by purely human standards, we must admit that a child prattles no less convincingly.' It is, perhaps, surprising that a man of such profound spiritual insight as Paul should have valued the gift of tongues highly, but it must be remembered that from the point of view of the Church, at any rate, he regarded it as inferior to 'prophecy'. 'Thank God I speak in "tongues" more than any of you; but in church I would rather say five words with my own mind for the instruction of other people than ten thousand words in a "tongue" ' (II *Corinthians* xiv. 19—Moffatt). When he refers to his 'understanding', I am sure he does not mean mere human reason without the light and leading of God. He seems to distinguish different degrees of inspiration in his utterances and writings. In I *Corinthians* ii he claims that the Holy Spirit imparts to him the deep wisdom of God which man's unaided intellect could never fathom, and then in inspired language he is able to communicate these 'secrets' to those who are spiritually mature enough to understand them. 'It is these things that we talk about, not using the expressions of the human intellect but those which the Holy Spirit teaches us, explaining spiritual things to those who are spiritual' (I *Corinthians* iii. 13—J. B. Phillips). But he is not always sure that he has the highest degree of inspiration, and so, in dealing with the celibate life, he says, 'and I *think* also that I have the Spirit of God' (I *Corinthians* vii. 40). And there are times when he will make no claim to inspiration at all. He expresses only his personal opinion and insists that it is to be judged as such: 'But to the rest speak I, *not* the Lord' (I *Corinthians* vii. 12 ff.).

Now inspiration will seldom, in most cases never, come to the preacher through what we may call abnormal experiences. There is, indeed, a significant change in the conception of inspiration within the Old Testament itself. By the time of the great prophets of the eighth century the frenzies and emotional orgies of the earlier 'schools of the prophets' have passed. It is true that revelation still comes occasionally through voice or vision. Much more frequently it comes to a man who has disciplined himself in quiet communion with God, and whose soul has been so purified by that communion that he looks out upon the world and life not through eyes as sinful and unseeing as those of the men around him but through the eyes of God Himself. Or, like Hosea, he reaches a deep insight into the nature of God and His ways with men as he broods upon the experiences of his own life. Many men besides Hosea have had unfaithful wives, but not many have lived so close to God that He has been able to reveal to them through their own yearning compassion that suffering, redeeming love which one day was to pour itself out on Calvary.

Inspiration will come to us, then, when we are receptive to God. In one of his novels Hugh Walpole makes an artist say, 'The whole duty of art is listening for the voice of God.' That is certainly the whole duty of the preacher. We shall not hear voices. We shall not see visions, for if Tertullian was speaking for his own age when he said that 'the majority of men learn God from visions', he was certainly not speaking for ours.

We shall receive our inspiration as we study the Word of God, as we read the books or listen to the conversations of those who have had great thoughts about God and man, not so that we may reproduce them in our next sermon but so that we may receive their insights into our own minds and hearts, and by using them to interpret our own experiences make them at last our own. Inspiration will come to us as we think about the needs of others and give ourselves to them with the kind of sympathy which makes other lives real. Above all, it will come as we gain in knowledge of ourselves—of the unfathomable depth of our own need, of our sins and failures, of our tangled motives, and, if God in His mercy delivers us from pride, it will come as we think gratefully of what grace has done in our own lives. For if we cannot, like Paul, do all things through Him that strengtheneth us, we can at least do a few.

I remember in my student days walking by the river at Oxford with that great Old Testament scholar, H. Wheeler Robinson, who was at that time the supervisor of my studies. He brought our talk round to the subject of preaching and asked me how I was faring. I told him I felt I was preaching too much about my own needs and the things that interested *me*. He replied, 'But what else should you preach about? What else could you preach about with conviction?' If I remember rightly over this distance of time, I meant that I felt I was preaching too much about the rather academic problems which interested me as a student and which I was aware were far removed from the needs of the men and women in the pews, even though at that time I knew little of what those needs really were. Of course, no preacher can be convincing unless he knows himself and speaks to his own condition. That great Scottish preacher, Alexander Whyte, once wrote to a minister who had asked his advice: 'Look into your own sinful heart, and back into your own sinful life, and around on the world full of sin and misery, and open your New Testament, and make application of Christ to yourself and your people; and, like Goodwin, you will preach more freshly and more powerfully every day until you are 80. . . . Don't hunger for books. Get a few of the very best, such as you already have, and read them and your heart continually; and no fear of your preaching. . . . Behmen "had no books, but he had himself", and though you had the whole Bodleian Library and did not know yourself, you would not preach a sermon worth hearing.'

Inspiration will come through the reading of great books— greatness is not, of course, to be measured by size—which call for effort and discipline before they become part of ourselves. It will not often come, I think, through a hurried turning of pages which will provide us with one or two ideas which can easily be produced on Sunday morning. And the good Doctor is right. Not even all the truly great books in the Bodleian Library will enable a preacher to make a sermon worth hearing if he does not know himself.

From all this it follows that inspiration will not generally come except at the cost of much toil and unfaltering honesty. Such a view of inspiration may seem to involve a contradiction in terms. People commonly mean by an inspiration a 'bright idea' or a 'brain wave' which seems to come suddenly from nowhere. A revelation may, indeed, seem to come in a flash even when we are not seeking it and our minds are on other things. But often, if we looked deeply into the matter, we should find that the way for this sudden illumination had been prepared over a long period of thought and questioning when no light at all was shining through our perplexity. I do not mean that sudden inspiration may not come to a preacher even at the most unlikely moment. The wind bloweth where it listeth—and when. Many a minister going about his pastoral work would claim that sometimes, when he has felt himself utterly at a loss, a word has been given him to say. It would be useless to tell him that this word, so wonderfully in season, was the fortunate result of much reading, and it could not have been the outcome of subconscious brooding on the situation since that was entirely unforeseen. He would reply that the word was not his at all, that it was given, that the Lord Himself had promised such aid to His disciples in their perplexity. When they found themselves before their judges, He said, words would be given them to speak. Why should such inspiration not be forthcoming in sick-room or study as well as in a law-court? And if God wants a thing said to an individual or a congregation, why should he not choose a man to say it? All that God needs is a receptive mind and spirit. Then He may enable a preacher to see a situation so clearly that he knows the thing that must be said—this and no other. It may be that God even gives the actual words. Such inspiration may come when a man toils in his study or when he stands before his congregation, and he may be carried out of himself by it. Henry Ward Beecher declared:

'There are times when it is not I that is talking; when I am caught up and carried away so that I know not whether I am in the body or out of the body; when I think things in the pulpit that I could never think in the study; and when I have feelings that are so different from any that belong to the lower or normal condition that I can neither regulate nor understand them. I see things and I hear sounds, and seem, if not in the seventh heaven, yet in a condition that leads me to apprehend what Paul said, that he heard things which it is not possible for a man to utter.'*

There are few of us who would dare to claim such an experience, but many a preacher would say that he has felt that he is being used by a power outside and yet within himself, and that his words are being given to him. But there is a danger here—the ever-present danger of self-deception. Hitler, ranting in frenzy before adoring multitudes, probably felt himself inspired. A preacher's feelings are no proof that he is inspired. We are seldom the best judges of our own inspiration. The reality of inspiration is proved by results—not by the drawing of crowds, but by the creative effect of the preaching in other lives.

The aim and purpose of preaching is now, I hope, clear. The preacher tries to bring about a personal encounter between God and the souls of his hearers. He seeks to lead every man to a place where he must meet God face to face and can find no way of evasion, no escape from the impact of God upon his mind and heart and conscience. When a man with ears to hear has listened to the faithful preaching of the Gospel, he stands naked and defenceless before the God who judges him, but who in His great mercy also forgives and empowers him.

But what am I doing? I am speaking as though preaching is, after all, only what a *man* does or seeks to do. But the true preacher seeks to do one thing, and one thing only—so to put himself in the hands of God that God may bring about the personal encounter through him. It is the glory of the preacher that the God

* *Patriotic Addresses*, p. 140.

who has His treasure in earthen vessels, and not very clean vessels at that, can use him so wonderfully. It is his shame that his lack of dedication so often frustrates God's purpose, and his personality is not a highway through which God comes to man and man to God, but a barrier between them.

CHAPTER TWO

The Personality of the Preacher – I

Like most ministers I have in my time read many books on preaching. Some of them were by giants of the pulpit who nevertheless were not very successful in communicating the secrets of their art; some were by men who, without being great preachers themselves, were able to write profoundly on the meaning and methods of preaching; a few—and these the most valuable— were by men who were masters of both the theory and practice of preaching. Of the books which fall into this last class I should without hesitation give first place to Phillips Brooks's *Yale Lectures on Preaching*. I know of no one who has had so many profound things to say about the preacher and his work.

At the outset Brooks gives his own definition of preaching. 'Preaching', he says, 'is the communication of truth by man to men. It has in it two essential elements, truth and personality. Neither of these can it spare and still be preaching . . . preaching is the bringing of truth through personality.'

'The bringing of truth through personality'—could anyone hope in half-a-dozen words better to express the essence of the matter? Truth is received into a human personality and through it is passed on to others. It is this double process of receiving and transmitting truth which constitutes the act of preaching. But we know, and bitterly in our own experience, that the process may be blocked. The obstacles may be between the preacher and God, so that His truth is not received, or between the preacher and the congregation, so that it is not communicated, or there may be so many hindrances that it is neither received no rcommunicated. The obstacles to communication may be in the congregation rather than in the preacher, but that we shall consider in a subsequent chapter. We are concerned now with the personality of the preacher as the channel of truth. So we must, with as much honesty as we can command, consider the personality of the preacher.

(1) No man should essay to be a preacher who has not received a genuine call to preach.

To some the call comes in a moment of sudden illumination, although the way for it may have been opened by a long period of conscious or unconscious preparation. There may have been months or years of anxious questioning and then comes the moment when all misgivings cease. Some preachers can point to the very place and time when the certainty of their call flashed upon them. So it was with John Henry Jowett. He had hoped to be a politician, and as a first step he had decided to become a lawyer. On the very day before his articles were to be signed, he met in the streets of Halifax his old Sunday School teacher who, hearing his plans for his future, looked grieved and said, 'I had always hoped you would go into the ministry.' That compelled Jowett to think again. He had felt himself drawn to the ministry, but had God *called* him to it? 'Years afterwards, recalling this crucial moment in his life, he said "the grip" came to him as he stood by the harmonium in the parlour at home. From that moment he had no hesitation. His course was clear.'

Many preachers could not pin-point any moment when 'the grip' came. They were conscious only of a growing conviction that preaching was their vocation and nothing else was possible for them. Looking back over the years, some of us can see now, as we could not see then, how the constraining hand of God was upon us. Luther once declared that from the vantage-point of after years he could see how God had led him like an old, blind horse. Perhaps it would be truer to say of some of us that we were frisky young colts and certainly were not aware of any leading. And, indeed, at any time we could have broken loose, for the constraints of God are not compulsions. But we can see now how some doors that we sought to enter were closed to us as though an invisible hand had softly yet firmly shut them, and others were unexpectedly opened. Whether the call was clinched with a sudden 'grip', or whether it came in a gradually maturing conviction with no moment of crisis, our emotions were mixed. There was joy that we believed ourselves chosen, but there was a sense of shrinking back from our mission. You will have noticed how the great prophets of the Old Testament almost to a man pleaded their unworthiness and would have escaped from the 'grip'. We might almost say that this is so normal a reaction to the call to preach that, if a man does not feel it, he had better ask himself whether the call really is of God.

I think it would be right to say that there are generally two elements in the call, although it is true that neither may be clearly present when a lad's thoughts first turn to the ministry. The idea may first enter his head because, for example, of the hero-worship he has for a beloved minister. That may be God's first line of approach, but much must happen before that youthful impulse can become a call with the seal of God upon it.

First, whoever would become a preacher must feel the needs of men until it becomes an oppression to his soul. I have sat for some years on a college committee which interviews men seeking admission to college, and I have noticed again and again that when they have been asked what turned their thoughts to the ministry they have replied that it was the need of the world and the conviction that Christ alone could meet it. If I were asked how the 'grip' came to me I should reply that it was through this sense of man's need, though it did not really take hold upon me until two or three years after I had entered college. I remember the moment as vividly as Jowett recalled standing by the harmonium. There was a transport strike in London, and I was walking through a drab street in the East End as the crowds were turning out of the public-houses. A drunken man reeled across in front of me and fell like a log in the middle of the road. There was no roar of traffic that night to drown the sickening, helpless thud of his fall. I could hear it for weeks and months afterwards. It symbolised for me the helplessness of foolish and sinful men for which there was no cure apart from God. I knew then how much men needed the Gospel, and perhaps for the first time I offered my life for the preaching of it. John R. Mott has said, 'The perception of a need and the consciousness of the ability to meet it, that constitutes a call.' No preacher is conscious of ability to meet the need, but he believes he has powers which God has given him to use in that way and no other. If he could use them in some other way and still be at peace with himself and God, the vocation of the preacher is not for him.

The second element in the call is what Paul terms 'the constraining love of Christ (II *Corinthians* v. 14)'. He does not mean his love for Christ, but Christ's love for him and for all men, the love which took Jesus to the Cross where one died for all. Faced with such a love, Paul could not but tell others about it, for he felt that the ministry of reconciliation had been given to him. But the awareness of what Christ had done for all would not have had such a constraining power if there had not been at the heart of it an intensely personal experience. You may be moved by the story of Jonathan Hall Edwards, one of the pioneers of X-rays, who, working in the city of Birmingham, lost his fingers, his hands, his arms in his efforts to relieve the sufferings of humanity. You are filled with admiration for such self-sacrifice. Yet you are not made humble and grateful as you would be if somebody endured such agony and mutilation in an heroic attempt to relieve *your* pain or save *your* life. You cannot be moved to the depths while you think only abstractly or in general terms. It was the deep conviction that 'the Son of God loved *me* and gave Himself up for *me*' which evoked Paul's gratitude and made him a preacher of the Gospel undaunted by hardships and persecutions, for he rejoiced in the sufferings which enabled him to feel that in some infinitesimal way he was sharing in the sufferings of Christ.

I have spoken of the way in which the call first comes to

a man, and you may think is suitable enough to young men contemplating the ministry or taking the first steps in it. But what has it to do now with those of us who have spent half a lifetime in this service and even those of us who are finishing the course? It has everything to do with us. We need to hear the call not once in youth but again and again all through our careers until God gives us our discharge. It is foolish to suppose that a man encounters all the perils of the ministry in his earliest years, and, having survived them by the grace of God, is safe until the day of his retirement. There are, in fact, temptations which lie hidden so that they may catch him in his later years when he may have been lulled into a false security. It is easy, for example, to become so accustomed to human need that we are no longer hurt or shocked by it. Middle-age often brings a dulling of the conscience, a cynical doubt as to whether things can ever be much different, a dislike of being disturbed. I ought to pray that when the call of man's need is drowned by the noises of the world, or I am too indolent or sleepy to heed it, I may hear again the dull thud of a helpless body on the tram-lines. And it is even easier through sheer familiarity to lose our sense of wonder at what Christ has done for us. We read about it, sing hymns about it, preach sermons about it, scores and hundreds of them, until the thing is in danger of becoming a habit. Virginia Woolf tells us that when Roger Fry was in Paris he used sometimes to spend a whole afternoon by himself in the Louvre. He would say, 'The old pictures must be seen again. I spent this afternoon in the Louvre. I tried to forget all I had ever heard or read about them and to look on them as though I had never seen them before. Only so can one make discoveries.' Again and again all through his ministry the preacher needs to go and stand before the Cross, trying to forget all he has ever heard or read about it, and looking upon it as though he were seeing it for the first time. Only so can he make discoveries.

The first qualification of the preacher is, then, that he has received a call to preach and that there is in him an urge which will not be denied. George Eliot makes Savonarola say, 'Without preaching I cannot live.' When a preacher finds that he can live equally well without preaching it is time for him to stop. I am anxious not to be misunderstood. Probably every preacher would confess that there are times when he has no urge to preach. My immediate predecessor at Carrs Lane, Leyton Richards, used to speak about 'the tyranny of the sermon'. No man, he said, ought to be expected to produce week after week and year after year two fresh sermons (perhaps with a mid-week address thrown in for good measure!) for the same congregation. Yes, any man who has to do that will inevitably feel at times stale and 'preached-out'. Or we may pass through moods of the soul or bitter experiences when we shall have to drive ourselves up the pulpit steps. We ought not to suppose at such times that we have no business to preach and that God has withdrawn His commission. I believe it often happens that when we are having most difficulty with ourselves we are most helpful to others. We are not always most convincing when our message comes easily and we can speak almost glibly. We may feel that we have had 'a good time', but few in our congregation may be the better for it. God may have used us much more effectively on a day when we have hardly known how to face our congregation, when it has been agony to preach at all, and we have come out of the pulpit with a sense of failure and a feeling that it would be a profound relief if we knew we should never have to preach again.

Times like these are a healthy discipline for the soul, and some of us, perhaps, need them, as Paul thought he needed his thorn in the flesh, to prevent us from being puffed up. The urge to preach is not dead; it will revive with new vigour. The preacher is in a more parlous condition when his urge is not diminished by a passing mood of the soul or a bitter experience but is eaten away by the slow corrosion of indifference. He feels no agony of mind or spirit. He goes on preaching, or perhaps we should say talking, in a pulpit because it has become a habit, and anyway, it is his means of livelihood. But he becomes less and less diligent in preparation, more casual in delivery, and has cynical things to say about the futility of preaching as though the cause were entirely in his congregation and not at all in himself. Such a man cannot really preach and should not pretend that he can. The fires have gone out.

We have thought at some length about the preacher's call. If the call is authentic and if a man responds to it with his whole heart, it may seem that there is nothing more to be said about the fitness of his personality for his vocation. But it may yet be worth while to remind ourselves of one or two essential qualities.

(a) Sincerity

I do not mean consistency between what a man professes and the quality of his everyday life. That is necessary in every Christian, and preachers do not fail more than others in this way. I am referring to intellectual and emotional integrity. This is a special obligation upon the preacher. Some of his hearers at least will invest him with authority because he speaks in a pulpit. They will regard him as having a specialised knowledge which they cannot share and religious feelings into which they cannot enter because they are not as spiritual as he.

Intellectual integrity does not mean that a preacher must be able to *prove* all that he asserts. It does mean that he must honestly believe it to be true. Dr L. P. Jacks says that there came a time in his ministry when, under the influence of something he had learned from Carlyle, he began to ask himself, 'How much in these sermons of yours represents what you really believe, and how much what you only want other people to believe?'

It is not sincere to preach what you only want others to believe, or what you think they would like to believe. Nor is it honest to preach what you can hold only because, not wishing to have your comfortable beliefs disturbed, you have closed your mind to the impact of new truth from whatever source it comes. We dare not be less honest than a scientist like T. H. Huxley, who used to talk about 'the fanaticism of veracity', or Darwin, who kept a note-book in which he jotted down things which seemed to contradict his theories because he knew he would be specially prone to forget them.

Sincerity does not mean that we must never have doubts. If it did most of us would have to stop preaching at once. When George Muller was asked if he had ever been troubled by doubt he thought for a moment and then replied, 'Yes, I once doubted for five minutes.' And Newman said that after entering the Roman Catholic Church he never had a moment's doubt. Most of us have never had such untroubled faith. We have doubted for much more than five minutes, and probably have doubted even the essentials of our faith.

These doubts may arise from many sources. Sometimes they have their origin in a guilty conscience. When we carry about with us an unrepented sin we may find ourselves doubting the very existence of God. What is more, we can find the most convincing intellectual reasons for our doubts! We are only trying to save our self-respect. If we can persuade ourselves that reason is not satisfied, we can think better of ourselves than we could if we were forced to admit that the thought of God is uncomfortable and even terrifying. It is not impossible that we shall succeed in conjuring up a little self-complacent pride in our intellectual acuteness and honesty. We shall do well to remember that most of us have a considerable facility in self-deception and that our minds are past-masters in the art of rationalising.

Doubts can arise also from such things as frustrations, slights and misunderstandings. Dr Bernard Hart tells of a patient of his who was a Sunday School teacher turned atheist. 'He insisted that he had reached this standpoint after a long and careful study of the literature of the subject, and he really had acquired a remarkably wide knowledge of religious apologetics. He showed considerable skill in producing a coherent and well-reasoned case. But the real cause of his atheism was the fact that the girl to whom he had been engaged had eloped with the most enthusiastic of his fellow Sunday School teachers.' May it not be that our doubts sometimes arise from some shock to our pride and self-esteem—a sharp criticism, a lack of appreciation, a failure in some project on which we had set our heart, the greater success of someone whom we regard, perhaps unconsciously, as a rival?

A depressed physical state is sometimes the source of doubt. In a post-influenza depression you can doubt everything! So you can when you are over-tired. Nearly all fatigue in the ministry is mental or spiritual in origin, even when we can hardly drag our bodies about. Many of us do not suffer from physical exhaustion but from lack of exercise. We should be all the better for a little muscular exertion every day suited, of course, to age and capacity! It would clear our minds wonderfully. But the neglect of our spiritual health is even more productive of doubts than disregard of the needs of our bodies. Slackness in prayer and study and the refusal to submit ourselves to spiritual discipline will bring forth a crop of doubts like weeds in an untended garden.

Finally, doubts, like loss of the urge to preach, may arise from some bitter experience of suffering. In the end we may preach with greater power and insight because these trials have come to us, but the immediate effect may be the feeling that we have nothing to preach because the faith which has hitherto sustained us has crumbled to pieces under the shock. Joseph Parker tells us in his autobiography (*Tyne Childe*) that up to the age of sixty-eight he had never had a doubt. He had never questioned the goodness of God, the Divinity of Christ, or anything vital to his faith. Then his wife died and, as it seemed to him, the faith by which he had lived and which he had preached to others, collapsed. 'In that dark hour I became almost an atheist. For God had set His foot upon my prayers and treated my petitions with contempt. If I had seen a dog in such agony as mine, I would have pitied and helped the dumb beast; yet God spat upon me and cast me out as an offence—out into the waste wilderness and the night black and starless.'

Sincerity does not mean that we must cease to preach when

doubts beset us, or that we must forthwith tell our congregations about them. Indeed, it would be wrong to shake the confidence of those whom we have been commissioned to build up in the faith by talking about doubts which may be no more than a passing phase. But if we hide our doubts from others we must not hide them from ourselves. We must face them, for only so shall we get the better of them. We must track them to their source. If they are genuinely intellectual doubts we must try to get the measure of them by study and by taking counsel with those more experienced or more learned. If they arise from some sin of pride or neglect, we must seek forgiveness and submit ourselves to spiritual discipline. If they are the effect of suffering we must take firm hold upon the fact that many before us have passed through darkness into a new light and a surer knowledge of God. 'I had heard of thee with the hearing of the ear, but now mine eye seeth thee.' But even in agony of spirit we must go on preaching and wait upon God. George Eliot, speaking of Savonarola, says that everybody who has to speak to the crowd must sometimes speak in virtue of yesterday's faith hoping that it will come back tomorrow. Thank God it generally does!

(b) Love

No man can preach who does not love people. He may produce learned dissertations, sound moral homilies or exquisite literary essays, but preach he will not. A preacher cannot, of course, love every individual member of his congregation in the same way as he loves his friends, for some of them he does not even know. But he can *care* for them all. 'Christianity taught us to care', said Von Hugel. 'Caring is the great thing. Caring matters most.' He can feel at least a little of the compassion which overwhelmed the heart of Christ when He saw the multitudes and felt their hunger and need as a burden on His own heart. A little while ago I was sitting on a committee interviewing young men who wanted to enter a theological college. There came before us one who had a brilliant academic record and was highly commended to us.

He had read a great deal of theology and was obviously interested in ideas. But I was not convinced that he was really interested in people. I am afraid I rather pressed the point, and after some thought he said, 'Oh yes. I am interested in people in a Kierkegaardian way.' I am not sure that I know what he meant, but I am quite sure that a preacher must care about people in Christ's way, whether that happens to be Kierkegaard's or not. I shall try to say something about what that kind of love means in a later chapter. Suffice it now to say that to suppose a man could preach without love would be against all logic. If God is love, how could His truth be brought to others through a personality that is not loving?

(c) Authority

There was a time when a preacher could reckon that he wielded a certain authority by virtue of his office. In Britain, at any rate, that is no longer true outside of the Roman Catholic Church. In my youth I knew an old lady who dropped a profound curtsy to her minister and a scarcely less deferential one to his wife, but she was born in the year that Queen Victoria came to the throne, and I think she was the last of her kind. Nor can a preacher reckon on the prestige that used to accrue from the fact that he was better educated than almost anyone in his congregation. Many a minister now has to recognise that there is probably somebody who knows more about every subject than he does with the possible exception of divinity—and some of us cannot be sure even about that! I, at any rate, can take nothing of the kind for granted. If I am guilty of a misquotation, I shall probably be corrected. If I confess that I do not remember the source of any words I use, I shall probably be informed of it by the first post on Monday morning. If, on my occasional incursions into science in search of an illustration—they are rare, for I long ago learned discretion in this matter—I fall into a technical error, it will inevitably be pointed out by somebody who has forgotten more science than I ever learned. Do not imagine that I am complaining, or that the whole congregation lies in wait with malice and spite to catch the preacher out. It is always done with kindliness and generally with a humour that delights and does not hurt. After all, it is evidence that some of the congregation are listening for some of the time, and it helps to keep the preacher careful and alert.

The authority which his hearers are prepared to acknowledge in the preacher does not reside, then, in his office or in the possession of superior academic qualifications. It is precisely the kind of authority which people recognised at once in Jesus. 'They marvelled because He taught as one having authority and not as the scribes.' These official religious leaders relied upon quotations from revered doctors of the law. Jesus did not cite precedents. He spoke simply and directly of things that He knew at first hand. His authority carried immediate conviction. It did not need the imprimatur of the seminary.

You will not suppose that I am decrying academic distinction or tilting at the ideal of 'a learned ministry'. I am only saying that the profoundest erudition in a preacher is no substitute for first-hand experience. Insight is not dependent on book-learning. Professor Herbert Butterfield, in his *Christianity and History*, says: 'When it comes to the essential things in human experience I think that a humble peasant may fall in love more profoundly and marry more successfully than some of the people who have been great scholars. Both in history and in life it is a phenomenon by no means rare to meet with comparatively unlettered people who seem to have struck profound spiritual depths and reached the real poetry of things—reached what I should regard as the very quintessence of the good life—while there are highly educated people of whom one feels that they are performing clever antics with their minds to cover a gaping hollowness that lies within. Some of the men who lived most fully and reflected most profoundly would not bear comparison with an average English schoolboy today if we judged them by their book-learning and scientific knowledge—of which Jesus Christ Himself must have had very little' (p. 115). Many a preacher, halting in speech, clumsy in gesture and lacking in scholarship, has carried immediate conviction because no one could doubt that he spoke of things which he knew at first-hand. 'What this parish needs', said Carlyle, 'is a minister who knows God other than by hearsay.' Yes, that is what every pulpit needs.

(d) Self-acceptance

It has been said of a famous actor that at sixteen he 'knew that he was precisely what he himself would have chosen to be if God had consulted him on the subject at his birth: he fully appreciated and approved what had been bestowed, and realised that he couldn't have done the job better himself. . . .' There are not many preachers who so fully appreciate and approve what has been bestowed. They feel they could have suggested a few improvements if they had been consulted at their birth! We are apt to wish that we had the impressive appearance, the silver voice, the flowing speech or some of the hundred and one other gifts which are listed in the biographies of the great preachers but which a short-sighted Providence denied to us.* There is no gainsaying that such endowments are assets to a preacher or to any other man who has to speak in public. Kinglake sat in the House of Commons for eleven years and often tried to make impressive speeches, but without any success. On one occasion he delivered a peroration which Mr Justin McCarthy described as 'remarkably eloquent and brilliant'. It failed to make any impression, for he had 'a thin voice and poor articulation'. The next night Sir Robert Peel (the second), with Kinglake's consent, 'wound up his own speech with Kinglake's peroration and brought the house down. Many a man preaching faithfully to a few people has felt that his material is as good as that of another who draws the crowds with his popular gifts. 'If only I had . . .' he thinks. Some men, unfortunately, become envious or cynical and decry popular gifts with the implication that they are glad they haven't got any! To use such gifts, like 'the clever antics of

* See introduction to Phillips Brooks's sermons for description of his personality.

the mind', to cover 'a gaping hollowness within' is a shameful thing, but it is hypocritical to pretend that there is no value in gifts of popular appeal if they help a man to 'get over' when he really has something to say. If we have them, let us thank God and pray to be delivered from the temptations they carry. If we have not, let us humbly accept ourselves and our limitations without wishing to be somebody else. But let us be sure what really are limitations and what are not. A man cannot by taking thought add one cubit to his stature or increase his actual intelligence. But he may learn how to improve the quality of his voice, how to rid himself of clumsy and irritating mannerisms and how to make the most of the mental powers he has. After all, it is said that Demosthenes was at first afflicted with a stammer. And Ellen Terry says that Sir Henry Irving 'at first had everything against him as an actor. He could not speak, he could not walk, he could not *look*. He wanted to do things in a part and he could not do them. His amazing power was imprisoned, and only after long and weary years did he succeed in setting it free.'

The plain fact is that many a man, by a determined struggle to overcome a handicap, has developed a gift to a degree of excellence never attained by one already so well endowed with it by nature that he supposed no discipline or effort was required of him. Self-acceptance must never be another word for indolence. But the real limitations, the things which cannot be changed, must be accepted without resentment. God does not require that we shall serve Him with the powers of another man but only to the utmost of our own. He 'doth not ask day labour, light denied'. In the sight of God no preacher will be judged by the number or the nature of his gifts, but only by the measure in which he has dedicated his whole personality, such as it is, to the work of preaching, so that through it truth may be brought to men for their salvation. 'No man', said Dr Forsyth, 'has any right in the pulpit in virtue of his personality or manhood in itself, but only in virtue of the sacramental value of his personality for his message.'

CHAPTER THREE

The Personality of the Preacher – II

It is much better to deal in positives than negatives, and it may seem wiser to concentrate our gaze wholly upon what a preacher ought to be than to turn our eyes upon what he all too often is. But we should not be dealing honestly with ourselves and our calling if we did not force ourselves to consider some of the faults which may vitiate a preacher's personality and work. Every vocation has its own peculiar tempations which nobody understands fully except those who are subjected to them. I suspect there are people in our congregations waging their daily warfare with 'the world', trying to keep their ideals bright amid the corrosive influences of society, and facing an unrelenting conflict of loyalties, who sometimes envy us what they suppose to be our easy and sheltered existence. Who are we, they ask, to exhort them? And those who have succumbed may be resentful, holding with good enough reason that we, too, might have fallen if we had been in their situations. But they are quite wrong when they suppose that we know nothing about temptation.

There are, in fact, few temptations which beset the man in the pew that do not also assault the man in the pulpit. They may come in slightly different guise, but essentially they are the same, and they are not made easier to resist by the fact that the minister has often to face them in solitariness and cannot turn to anybody for the understanding and help which others seek from him. The temptations of 'the word', of 'human society as it organises itself apart from God', find their way into the study and the pulpit by employing every refinement of subtlety. If temptations came in too crude a form we might recoil from them in horror and, as

34

Newman said, our greatest security against sin lies in being shocked at it. Sometimes–God forgive us!—we may be conscious hypocrites, but usually before it can get its way with us temptation has to lure us into self-deceit and into seeing a fault as a virtue, or at least persuade us that we are acting from the highest motives. The urge to preach, which we have said every preacher must have, may arise from, or be reinforced by, motives far removed from those which we have found to be the right ones.

(*a*) Dare we ignore, for example, the craving for power? That, as some of us tell our congregations at least twice a month, is at the back of so many of the world's problems—racial, international, industrial and even domestic. We had better beware lest we be so busy exposing and denouncing the lust for power in others that we miss its more subtle manifestations in ourselves. Browning's Bishop was honest enough to admit that he was not immune:

> There's power in me and will to dominate
> Which I must exercise; they hurt me else.

The devil likes hunting big game, but he is not averse to smaller prey! If he can beguile a bishop with the power and glory of his office, that is a notable triumph; but if a minister in even the humblest sphere can be induced to make the most of his limited opportunities for exulting in power, that is a victory not to be despised. We shall be lulled into a false sense of security if we suppose that the urge to power is a serious temptation only to those who have spectacular chances to gratify it.

A minister may feel the lure of power in his ordinary relationships with his people. Some men there are whose will to dominate openly shows itself in their attempts to become dictators in their own churches. I have known some to succeed in an astonishing way, but I think the lot of the man who aspires to absolute power is harder than it used to be. In England, at any rate, the minister is seldom put upon a pedestal, nor is he allowed to climb on to one of his own volition. The congregation sometimes takes firm hold of the truth that a minister is the servant of all, but they interpret that to mean that, as the one full-time paid worker of the church (as he generally is), he is a handy man to do the chores. (It is right enough that a minister should not think that he is above the most menial task, and in an emergency he will turn his hand to anything, but he is not to be at everybody's beck and call for jobs that should be the responsibility of others.) It is just as likely that the minister will be dictated to as that he himself will be a dictator. Nevertheless, the will to dominate may be present when it cannot be exercised and then, as the bishop said, it may hurt. Its frustration may show itself in irritability, bad temper, resentment and all kinds of useless things which are quite different from the calm strength of a man whom people give up trying to bully because they can make no impression upon him. There is a place in the life of the Christian minister for leadership humbly accepted as a stewardship; there is none for the will to dominate. It is the will that is wrong even if circumstances prove too strong for it.

In his pastoral work a minister may encounter more subtle perils of the desire for power. Here, too, satisfaction is often easier to achieve because his quest for power in the privacy of these personal relationships is not open and challenging like an attempt to dominate a church. Further, there are people who will willingly offer submission in order to satisfy their own emotional needs. They want to be told what to do; they want somebody to run their lives for them. The very fact of receiving people's confidence and of holding their secrets gives to some ministers an elation which comes less from the sense of being used to help others than from the feeling of power, although they do not, of course, intend to use the power in any dishonourable way. Not infrequently a person in emotional difficulties becomes strongly attached to a minister and clings to him in complete dependence. If this does not become embarrassing, he may find it very gratifying, since it may help him to feel that he is a strong, dependable personality upon whom others may lean. Then he may be unwilling to alter the relationship by helping his 'patient' to achieve independence and stand on his own feet.

I have said so much to indicate that the craving for power may tempt a minister in his study or in the homes of his people, but here we are chiefly concerned with him in the pulpit. The man who has a great gift of speech may have a running fight with this temptation all through his ministry. If he can make a crowd—it need not be a very big one—hang upon his words while he sways their emotions and draws from them what response he will, he may feel that he has them completely in his power. Some speakers and preachers have confessed that there is a kind of intoxication in this experience. There is also the gratification of being able to stand in a pulpit *above* a congregation and lay down the law without fear of contradiction. That may come afterwards, but it can be forgotten in the security of the pulpit. Even the fact that the preacher is lifted up in the pulpit above the congregation is not without significance. Mussolini's ego would probably have been much less inflated if he had been compelled to play the demagogue from ground level instead of on a balcony high above the crowd in the piazza!

The sense of power does not come only to preachers whose technique is designed to play upon the emotions of a congregation. Dr J. D. Jones of Bournemouth was a quiet and thoughtful preacher, who always read his sermons and never indulged in orgies of emotional oratory, yet he once confessed to his people: 'Yes, I will be frank and say I found a certain love of fame in my heart. I found a certain pride in reputation in my heart. I found a certain glorying in the power this pulpit gives me in my heart.'

(*b*) Closely allied to the craving for power is the love of praise. It is natural and right to take pleasure in praise when it is sincerely given and justly deserved. The man who loudly and defiantly proclaims that he doesn't care what *anybody* thinks of him is trying to cover up the fact that he has an even stronger desire than usual for approval, and at the same time to protect himself in case he does not get it. If his words could be taken at their face value it would mean that he had only contempt for his fellows, and that would be nothing to his credit. Many ministers who are doing good work and preaching faithfully do not get the praise they merit. Others, especially 'popular' preachers, get more than they deserve. Sometimes it passes beyond praise into adulation. There is always the danger that a man who receives a great deal of praise may come to depend upon it. If he does not get the usual full measure he may almost fly into a panic, believing that he has lost his touch, is a dismal failure, is finished, and so on. A liberal infusion after the next sermon will, of course, generally restore the balance and give him back his confidence. So able and distinguished a man as the late Bishop Hensley Henson detected in himself something of this irrational craving for praise. After he had preached he says, 'Woodbridge, his brother, and the naval lad, were good enough to express their approval of the discourse, which I "lapped up" with the gusto with which preachers absorb the hollow compliments of their hearers.'

The danger is that a preacher may become a praise addict. He must have it at any cost and from any source as others must have alcohol. The alcohol addict, it may be, once had a fine, discriminating palate for choice wines, but now his main desire is to get intoxicated, and he cannot be particular about the quality of the stuff that produces the effect. The desire for praise may so get the better of a preacher that he can no longer distinguish flattery and 'hollow compliments' from sincere gratitude and approval of a piece of work well done. As an alcoholic will plead for spirits, the praise addict, though not so abjectly, will angle for compliments, and hope by depreciating his work to provoke someone into assuring him of its brilliance.

The preacher, then, can be humbly grateful when one of his hearers grips his hand and says 'That helped me', or when one whose judgement he can respect tells him 'That was well done.' But he must be on guard against the excessive love of praise which can grow so insidiously that it evades notice. It may have its roots either in vanity or in a sense of inferiority that needs constant reassurance. Its moral significance is different in the two cases, but its ultimate effects may be much the same. The vain man accepts flattery because he has first flattered himself. Bernard Shaw once said, 'I am proof against all illusions except those that flatter me.' Those are the illusions which it is most painful to discard, but they ought to be the first to go, not the last.

Even those who are not praise addicts are in danger of lowering their standards if they fall into the habit of accepting praise too readily. A preacher may know well enough that his sermon is ill-prepared and far below his best work, but there may be no lack of hollow compliments. After a little of this he will be thinking that he can be a successful preacher without the thought and care that he once put into his sermons. He will be wise to ask himself whether he still occasionally receives the restrained praise, so unlike effusive flattery, of those whose judgement bears some weight.

> Like Verdi when, at his worst opera's end,
> (The thing they gave at Florence;—what's its name?)
> While the mad houseful's plaudits near out-bang
> His orchestra of salt-box, tongs and bones,
> He looks beyond the roaring and the wreaths
> Where sits Rossini patient in his stall.

But the preacher must look for the final verdict beyond even the most searching human judgement to the God who called him to be a preacher, and who alone knows how faithfully he has done his work.

(c) Perhaps we have put the cart before the horse in thinking about the love of praise before the dangers of self-display. Obviously the two are closely related. The man who wants to keep himself entirely out of the public eye is not likely to become a praise addict, but neither is he likely to become a preacher. I once remarked in the senior common room of a theological college that every minister must face the fact that the desire for self-display was one of the motives which took him into the ministry. There was a pained silence which was broken by the only layman present. 'It's right, you know,' he said. 'Whether you like it or not, it's right.' Of course it is. How could anyone who had *no* liking for self-display ever climb into a pulpit? Unless it can be said of us, as of St Francis Xavier, that we would like to reform the world without our own existence being known, we shall do well to admit that we are not wholly without an appetite for self-display. Then we can begin to take the measure of it.

In the case of the preacher there is a paradox: he must express his personality to the full while submitting to its total negation.

Preaching is 'truth through personality', but if the personality obtrudes itself the work of preaching is hindered. This is true even if the preacher is not indulging in *conscious* self-display. If people are thinking how clever, how eloquent, how witty or how learned the preacher is, there is no personal encounter with God. They cannot see God for the man in the pulpit. It is even worse when his hearers say, 'He is a born actor. He could have made a fortune on the stage.' If a minister has a dramatic gift he may use it to make him a more effective preacher. But if it is not controlled, if it is not subordinated to the purpose of preaching, but instead is exploited to draw attention to the preacher, there is need of the drastic surgery which Jesus had in mind when He said, 'If thine hand cause thee to stumble cut it off and cast it from thee.' Dr Jowett tells us that when he was in Northfield he went early one morning to conduct a camp meeting away in the woods. The camp dwellers were two or three hundred men from the Water Street Mission in New York. At the beginning of the service prayer was offered for him, and the prayer opened with the inspired supplication: 'O Lord, we thank Thee for our brother. Now blot him out!' And it continued, 'Reveal Thy glory in such blazing splendour that he shall be forgotten.' A great British preacher, Dr John Watson ('Ian Maclaren'), summed up the matter thus: 'As it now appears to me, the chief effect of every sermon should be to unveil Christ, and the chief art of the preacher to conceal himself.'

The other half of the paradox is that the preacher must express himself. The reason why some men of undoubted intellectual ability and spiritual insight are not effective preachers is that they cannot liberate their own powers in the act of preaching. Some are full of inhibitions, shut in upon themselves and never able even in the most congenial surroundings to 'let themselves go'. Their lack of freedom in the pulpit is part of their personality-problem as a whole, and they are not likely to make effective preachers unless they can break down the emotional barriers which thwart self-expression in every part of their lives. There are other men who are lively and unaffected in normal life, but as soon as they mount the steps of a pulpit they become strained and tense, showing many signs of anxiety, unable to be themselves, and possibly adopting a professional pose complete with parsonic unction and the clerical voice. There may be many causes for this painful transformation, some of them rooted in deep-seated emotional conflicts which call for skilled help if they are to be resolved. They are outside the scope of this book, and anyway they are beyond my competence. But sometimes the reason may be less obscure. The preacher may be so concerned about himself and the impression he is making that anxiety prevents him from being himself at all. He must remind himself that he is not in the pulpit to impress people with his own personality or to score a resounding triumph. He is there to be used by God. When he ceases to be anxious about himself he will be himself. On the other hand, there are men who are shy, diffident and emotionally inhibited who, once they are in a pulpit, achieve a liberation which transforms them. It may be that they have surrounded themselves with a wall of reserve because they lack confidence and security. The authority which the pulpit gives them supplies the necessary assurance, and having emerged into the limelight from the obscurity they seek, but do not really desire, they are able to throw off their inhibitions.

Self-expression, of course, means expressing one's own self and not trying to express somebody else's. Every great preacher who has striking individual traits has his imitators. It is said that pale copies of Joseph Parker were to be found in pulpits all over England. Some imitators are, perhaps, so despondent about their own personalities that they suppose they can only succeed if they can graft on a few striking characteristics, or even eccentricities, belonging to another. In the original these things may be genuine expressions of personality and therefore may have value; in the imitator they never become part of the personality, but remain merely ludicrous accretions. To learn from a master how to develop one's own personality is one thing; to attempt to copy his is quite another. And if the motive for imitation is not a despairing attempt to make good the deficiencies of one's own personality in order to become a more effective preacher, but merely to attract attention to oneself, the effort is not only futile but despicable.

Self-expression does not mean, in the pulpit any more than in morals, giving free rein to every impulse and, in general, doing exactly as you please. The stronger a man's impulses and passions the greater his possibilities of good, but the greater also his need for self-discipline lest they should prove his undoing. And the preacher with great and striking gifts must keep a check upon them or they may get out of hand. I think of a preacher who has a tremendous power of playing upon the emotions of an audience or congregation. I have seen him—not, for we must be fair, in a sermon, but in an address—keep his audience almost continuously in fits of laughter. They hung upon his words, waiting for the next 'crack'. But he was not there merely as an entertainer and did not intend to be regarded as one, for he was a man of serious purpose and evangelical fervour. Yet when he meant to have done with the fooling and to begin to treat his subject and his hearers seriously, they were not in the mood for it. He had gone too far; he had let his gift run away with him. They assumed that he was still making jokes and were sure they must be good ones even if they couldn't quite see the point! So they still laughed, and the good man found himself in the embarrassing position of pleading to be taken seriously. Another preacher may find that the gift of fluent speech is a pitfall, for he may use an abundance of words to conceal a paucity of matter, and may succeed with the less thoughtful among his congregation. Another, who uses vivid and forceful language, may have to learn to bridle his tongue. I believe that great and saintly preacher, G. A. Studdert Kennedy ('Woodbine Willy'), regretted that his one-time habit of using slang in the pulpit earned him a reputation for being unconventional which obscured the Gospel he longed so passionately to proclaim. The man with a poetic imagination must take care lest he begin to weave fancies for the sheer delight of it instead of to illuminate truth. And the preacher who can present an argument forcefully must be on his guard lest he should exult so much in the force of his blows that he tries to bludgeon the minds of his hearers and ends by provoking resistance. In short, every power carries with it the need for self-discipline. The more luxuriant the growth the greater the need for pruning if there is to be good fruit. Self-expression in the pulpit means the disciplined training and the employment to the full of all the gifts we have received for the sole purpose of setting forth the Gospel we are called to preach.

Here, perhaps, we may put the question: How far is a preacher justified in using deliberate artifices which may appear spontaneous but which have, in fact, been carefully thought out and even rehearsed beforehand? Let me illustrate the point by examining a story—probably apocryphal—which has been told of Jowett. It is said that a commercial traveller whose business brought him to Birmingham, went to Carrs Lane to hear the famous preacher, and was much impressed. In particular, he was gripped by a moment in the sermon when the preacher seemed to be wrestling with an idea which he could not quite express. The right word would not come to mind. With a gesture as though he were groping for it, he said, 'I want a word! I want a word!' Then at last his hand was upon it and he plucked it out of the air. The word was found! Now, soon afterwards in another city the traveller saw a placard announcing that Jowett was to visit the place. This was an opportunity not to be missed, and having suitably extolled the virtues of the preacher, he persuaded another traveller to accompany him to the service. He was somewhat taken aback when Jowett began to deliver the same sermon as at Carrs Lane. However, all went well until the preacher started to grope in the air and say, 'I want a word!' At that the traveller jabbed his companion in the ribs, muttered, 'I'm getting out of here', and made for the door. Outside his astonished friend asked him, 'Why did you rush out like that?' 'Couldn't stand it', he replied. 'I knew what the blooming word was!'

Now Jowett was deliberately employing an artifice—call it 'a trick of the trade' if you will—in order to create an impression upon his hearers. He also knew what the word was, and always had known, for he prepared his sermons to the last detail and wrote them out in full. I have heard it said that if this story is true Jowett was dishonest. But I am ready to defend him. He was, I do not doubt, repeating and dramatising what actually did happen when he was preparing the sermon. He *did* search for exactly the right word, and he could not rest until he had found it. For the study of words and the precise use of them was a passion with him. 'Words', says his biographer (who does not tell the story!), 'were the implements of his craft as a preacher, and no artist studied his pigments with purer delight. All the fine gradations of nouns and verbs, adverbs and adjectives yielded their secrets to his scrutiny and enabled him to wed the inevitable adjective to the inescapable noun with infallible felicity. A fine phrase thrilled him; a delicate *nuance* set him tingling. Once when talking to me of his passionate delight in word study, he likened his hobby to Henry Ward Beecher's habit of carrying precious stones in his pocket so that in odd moments he might hold them in the sunshine and watch the multi-coloured rays flash from their facets. "I do something like that," said Jowett, "only with words." '

The point is this: although Jowett was deliberately employing an artifice, he was not pretending an experience which had never come to him; he was not feigning an emotion that he had never felt. And he was not seeking to impress his congregation with his own ingenuity, ability as an actor, or anything else. He was employing the device in an honest attempt to rivet upon the minds of his hearers an essential part of his message. Because they would recall his search with its accompanying gesture, they would recall the word and all it stood for much more vividly than they would if he had merely said it as one word among many. The conclusion surely is that a preacher may employ an 'artifice' if it is honest, and if it intended to focus attention upon his message and not upon himself. The moment he begins to play to the gallery by eloquence, by a display of emotion which is not genuine, by a parade of learning, or by any 'trick of the trade', it is time for him to take himself in hand and remind himself that the chief art of the preacher is to conceal himself.

(d) The preacher's message may be distorted by his need to satisfy some emotional need of his own. In his valuable book *Psychology for Ministers and Social Workers*, Dr H. J. S. Guntrip examines this matter in some detail and I am deeply indebted to him here. He deals particularly with three types of preaching: the denunciatory, the dogmatic authoritarian and the popular topical.

Of denunciatory preaching he says: 'Moral indignation has its roots in our struggles against evil in ourselves. We tend to wax hottest against those evils towards which we ourselves have secret and repressed tendencies. Moreover, we often find a pleasure in moral indignation and denunciation that we would be slow to admit. It provides a socially permissible outlet for our own aggressive feelings. The *belligerent* [italics mine] pacifist enjoys his verbally militant attacks on warmongers. The sexual prude finds an only thinly disguised pleasure in fiercely condemning the licentious behaviour of the times, for that gives an opportunity of talking sex, if not of acting it. No one condemns the totalitarian Nazi more destructively than the equally totalitarian Communist. These things are known to us all, but we fall into the trap more easily than we like to admit. It is so much easier to project our faults on to other people than to face them in ourselves and undergo a change of character.'*

When a preacher has an inner conflict because his whole self is not behind his vocation, he may, if the inner rebel is too strong, 'be driven by a need for strict self-discipline and even self-attack, which he unconsciously expresses by working it off on his congregation in the form of preaching an intolerantly exacting idealism or a constant harping on the themes of sin and repentance'.†

The dogmatic-authoritarian type of preaching may be a way of sublimating a lust for power. 'A man who, in private life, is intolerant of contradiction and disagreement, who gets heated in argument against those who will not accept his views, who must always be right, who identifies himself with fixed opinions and is not prepared to change or learn, can find an easy rationalisation for all these stubborn, resistant, and at bottom anxious attitudes by *identifying himself* [italics mine] with an unchallengeable Word of God which he proclaims, and for which he demands unquestioning acceptance from his hearers.'‡

The popular-topical preacher may 'bask in the hearty approval of his own congregation by reiterating for them their own views, and, maybe, conventions and prejudices; or he may take the other line, and secretly pat himself on the back for his courage and boldness in "speaking out plainly" on matters on which he knows members of his congregation will disagree with him'.§

* H. J. S. Guntrip, *Psychology for Ministers and Social Workers*, pp. 72 f.
† Ibid., p. 74.   ‡ Ibid., pp. 75 f.   § Ibid., p. 77.

I am afraid that taken as a whole this may seem to be a rather discouraging chapter. The way of the preacher, it appears, is beset with temptations. And so it is—more than any other way of life that I can imagine. We have to face our temptations, and if we are to do that successfully we have first to face ourselves. It is so easy to avoid dealing honestly with our own personal problems by preaching to other people about theirs. That we dare not do. We must come face to face with ourselves in the presence of God, where we shall be stripped even of the last illusion that flatters us. With ruthless honesty we must try to know ourselves and our own motives. Do not imagine that I am pleading for a life of constant introspection. If a man cannot enter his study or his pulpit without prying every time into his motives and deploring his unworthiness, he will soon unfit himself for preaching or any other useful work. Introspection, as Bishop F. R. Barry once said, is like castor oil—good if used occasionally for purging when something is wrong, but not very nourishing if taken as a substitute for breakfast coffee. Even when searching self-examination reveals that we have mixed motives, as it certainly will, it does not follow that we must abandon our vocation or suppose that we were mistaken and never had a call to preach. Dr J. A. Hadfield, whose lectures first awakened me in my student days to the importance of psychology for the personality and work of the minister, has some wise words to say on this subject: 'If a man originally became a preacher to gratify the instinct of self-display, why should he abandon his calling on the discovery of this? If he has a strong instinct of display, how better can he use it than by illuminating great truths and moral principles? And if he can use his instinct of self-display in such a service, why not recognise and enjoy its use? The recognition of such motives brings happiness and increases power.' He adds as a footnote: 'It is an extraordinary fact that, although I have analysed a large number of clergymen in whom the instincts of self-display or self-importance, and sometimes self-righteousness, have played so large a part, in no case has any one of them felt it necessary to abandon his calling, but they have returned with fuller, stronger life to use and enjoy this instinct in the service of their work.'* These self-regarding impulses, which once mingled with our genuine love of God and man to create the irresistible sense of a 'call', must be accepted by us and then offered to God that He may control and use them. They are not safe when they are in our hands alone. As we offer them to Him we shall be cleansed from narrow and petty selfishness. But until our sanctification is complete—which will not be in this life— our love of self-display or praise or power will sometimes get the better of us, and then we shall preach, not for God's glory, but our own. It is a comforting, yet humbling, thought that God sometimes uses us when we are at our worst to make us helpful to others. I cannot tell how it happens, but I know it does. If it were not so, I should more often be in despair.

* J. A. Hadfield, *Psychology and Morals*, p. 74.

CHAPTER FOUR

The Art of Communication

George Bernard Shaw said rather cruelly of the poet, W. E. Henley, that he was a tragic example of a man with imposing powers of expression and nothing important to express. There are preachers of the same kind. There are others who have a great deal worth expressing, but they cannot 'get it over'. They have never mastered the art of communication.

Communication by public speech is an art if, as my dictionary affirms, an art is 'practical skill guided by rules'. It is true that some successful speakers and preachers have never given a thought to the rules. They don't know how they do it. They achieve their results by intuition, by an unerring feeling for what is 'just right' at any moment. Every art has its rules and every successful artist obeys at least some of them, consciously or unconsciously. A man may, of course, be so much a slave of rules that he can hardly be called an artist at all. He is not more than a mechanic. The true artist can combine individuality with respect for the principles of his art. It would be a dreadful thing if the rules of the art of communication were so rigid that all preachers had to conform to a single pattern. Some preachers seem to have been effective because they were 'characters' who had scant respect for any rules. I think it would often be found that they did, in fact, observe the rules, though they had probably never given them a moment's thought. In any case a genius or 'character' may have such unusual power of compelling attention that he may succeed even if he does flout most of the rules. But a mere eccentric, especially one who deliberately cultivates his own oddities or copies those of the

49

great, has little power to compel anything except boredom or disgust.

So to the rules:

(1) *The preacher must be sensitive to his congregation*

There are preachers who seem to have no 'feeling' for a congregation. They are emotionally detached. They might just as well be talking in an empty auditorium or to any other collection of people. They are quite unaware of the reactions of the people in the pews. If the congregation is bored, if some of them are fidgeting, some looking at their watches, some sleeping or turning glazed eyes to the pulpit, it is all the same—they will never notice. Some preachers, if they do observe their effect upon their hearers, are quite indifferent to it, like an eighteenth-century curate, Charles Churchill, of Rainham, who said, 'Sleep at my bidding crept from pew to pew.' Sometimes indifference is due to failure to take the vocation of preaching seriously, sometimes to pride which says, 'If they don't like it, they can lump it.' These faults, we may hope, are rare. Much more often the preacher has never realised that a personal relationship can be established even with a congregation whom he has never seen before. Perhaps he is interested in ideas and not in people, in which case it is doubtful whether the Lord ever meant him to be a preacher at all. Or perhaps he is aware of the need for making sympathetic contact with his congregation but doesn't know how to go about it.

One of the cardinal rules here is: look at your congregation. A fellow-student of mine had a book with the extraordinary title *The Use of the Eyes in Preaching*. I did not read it, but it might have contained some sound advice, though how anybody could have written a whole book on the subject passes my comprehension! The eyes are the chief means of establishing contact and confidence between human beings. According to Konrad Lorenz, if you are trying to establish friendly relations with a dog, you should give him a side-long look; you should not fix both your eyes on him, for he will regard that as a sign of hostility. But we are dealing with human beings, not dogs! When we talk to a person in friendship and confidence we look into his eyes. We do not stare or glare at him, we do not 'fix' him, but neither do we let our eyes wander all over the room—down to the floor, up to the ceiling, out at the window, anywhere except to his face. Some preachers who do not rivet their eyes upon the reading desk, or sweep them, like searchlights, over the heads of the people, or fix them with a glassy stare on some point at the back of the church, nevertheless do not *see* the congregation. They see a collection of bodies, but they do not see the people as individuals. I believe a preacher can train himself to 'see' a congregation. It is worth while to take an opportunity earlier in the service to study some of the faces. This can be done during the singing of a hymn or the anthem so long as he does not systematically review the congregation row by row in a way that will inevitably suggest he is counting heads or mentally marking a register. If the congregation is unknown to him he can try to read what some of the faces are saying and what needs they are revealing. Even if he happens to be wrong, in every case he will at least have made himself realise that he is dealing with real people. If he is facing his own congregation there will be many with whom he has had pastoral relationships. He does not need to conjecture their needs. He already knows some of them, and is reminded of them as he looks into their faces. If a minister accustoms himself to 'take in' a congregation in this way, he will probably continue to look at them while he preaches. But he must be careful how he uses his eyes during the sermon. He must not 'fix' an individual or a group of people with a prolonged stare. If he does, they will become self-conscious and think he is 'preaching at' them. Every preacher who looks directly at his hearers can recall times when somebody has said, 'I know you meant that for me because you looked straight at me when you said it.' In vain he protests that he did not have anyone in mind and did not deliberately look anywhere at that moment.

Sometimes, of course, the mild impeachment, whether made with good humour or resentment, is the symptom of a guilty conscience in the hearer, but it would be a bad thing if the preacher's unconscious habit of fixing people with his eye led to the conclusion that he was generally training his artillery in the direction of his gaze. There would be uncomfortable wriggling in the target area and a surreptitious turning of heads in other parts of the church to see who was in the danger zone! To avoid these *contretemps* the preacher should move his eyes from group to group, as he naturally will if he is talking *to* them and not merely talking in their presence, but not so quickly as to suggest furtiveness or nervousness. When he is engaged in a piece of 'straight speaking' it is particularly important to look steadily into the eyes of the congregation, yet without glaring at them.

If, then, a preacher looks at his congregation with seeing eyes, he is able to gauge the effect of his words, and if, in addition, he has freedom of utterance—we shall come to this later—he will often be able to adjust his presentation or delivery as may be necessary.

(2) *The preacher must help the congregation to feel friendly towards him*

The problem is already partly solved when a minister is preaching to his own people who know and love him. The confidence and affection between a minister and his own congregation sometimes mean that a 'poor' preacher is effective with them, whereas he would make little impression on strangers. On the other hand, if his congregation do not like him, nothing that he can do when he has mounted the pulpit steps will create the relationship favourable to the imparting and receiving of truth.

It is not to be expected that every individual can be induced to like any preacher. Quite irrational, and even unconscious, factors may create resistances. A man may dislike a preacher because there is a resemblance to someone against whom he has felt antagonism, perhaps long ago in childhood. A woman who has been dominated by a parent or husband may have an antipathy to all preachers because 'they lay down the law'. But, in the main, the congregation must feel friendly at the beginning of the sermon, even if some become estranged before the end because they have been forced to face up to uncomfortable truths.

The creation of friendliness is largely in the hands of the preacher. The initiative is with him. If he is genuinely interested in his congregation, is glad to be with them and honestly desires to serve them, they will sense his friendliness. If he is aloof and bored and obviously wishing himself somewhere else, they will sense that too. I think of a man whose smile can tell a congregation at once that he has taken them to his heart. But if nature has not endowed you with such a smile as the expression of genuine feeling, you will never be able to cultivate one by practising in front of a mirror! You will probably achieve nothing more than the inane expression of a man who has determined as a matter of professional duty to 'love' his congregation for the next hour or so.

The shortest and surest way a preacher can take to destroy the goodwill of a congregation is to arouse in their minds a suspicion that he is adopting a pose of superiority. Sometimes the matter is beyond suspicion—the assumption of superiority is written all over the man. The most obnoxious way of revealing it is by 'talking down' to the congregation. This is certain to arouse resentment. 'Talking down' is, of course, quite different from speaking simply. Everybody, except the intellectual snob, welcomes simplicity in the pulpit. Nor are we necessarily 'talking down' if we assume a great deal of ignorance about the Bible and theology and many other things, and so begin our exposition or instruction farther back than is necessary for the few well-informed members. It is, again, only the intellectual snob who will not appreciate the need for this. In its proper context a rebuke to a congregation for its neglect to study the Bible or Christian doctrine may be salutary, but the preacher then assumes that his hearers have the necessary intelligence for this discipline if they had also the will to undertake it. The essence of 'talking down' is the implied suggestion that grown-up people are lacking in intelligence, at any rate compared with the preacher, and therefore must be treated as children or half-wits. (Actually nobody is quicker than a child to detect and resent being 'talked-down to'.)

Even more galling is the assumption of moral superiority? The only man with a right to make such an assumption will never do it, for he is the true saint and a mark of sainthood is humility. The preacher should know his own heart too well to permit himself any air of superiority. He should have a healthy fear lest, having preached to others, he himself should be a castaway. A congregation hates 'being done good to', and will give short shrift to a preacher who condescends to them. If he is to stand on a moral or spiritual eminence, it is they who must put him there, and of him it will be said that 'he wist not that his face shone'. For his part, he will make people feel that he stands not above them, but beside them, identifying himself with them in their weaknesses and sins, and that he is never more one with them than when he speaks in exhortation or rebuke.

Equally disastrous is the use of sarcasm which, in common with 'talking down', betrays an attitude of contempt. The word is said to be derived from a Greek verb meaning 'to tear flesh like dogs', and its lacerating tooth can inflict poisoned wounds which are slow to heal and often leave a permanent scar. Some preachers have made effective use of a gentle kind of irony, which is good-humoured and has nothing vicious about it, but it must be used sparingly, if at all, for simpler souls may mistake it for sarcasm. Irony needs a delicate touch, and the preacher who is not endowed with that had better eschew the use of it altogether. Nor is the preacher the best judge of whether he has it or not. What seems to him gentle irony may strike others as heavy sarcasm!

Aggressiveness is another thing which has a 'putting-off' effect. It is, of course, quite different from direct, forceful speaking. Aggressiveness suggests that a man is unsure of himself or his message. A preacher may give way to it when he is dealing with a particular subject in order to satisfy his own unconscious emotional need, when he is not intellectually convinced of the truth of what he is saying and is trying to persuade himself and others by his own vehemence, or when he is aware that his words may provoke dissent and hopes by a show of ferocity to overawe the opposition. He will probably win the enthusiastic approval of those whose opinions and emotional needs are like his own, but he does not need to convince them, and, for the rest, he will inevitably defeat his own purpose. He will fail even with the open-minded, who will be alienated by a man who has so little respect for the personalities of others that he is prepared to try to bludgeon them into agreement or make them feel fools.

A less serious menace to friendliness, but one to be noted, is the failure to correct small irritants in speech or manner. Incessant or pointless movements of the hands, slovenliness, which suggests a lack of respect for the hearers, the continual use of the same words or phrases, a pompous manner (probably due to inferiority), an unctuous clerical voice, and dozens of other things may get on the nerves of a congregation. The cure for them is a candid friend—this role is often played by the minister's wife!—and the humility to heed and profit by advice.

(3) *The preacher must make the congregation feel at ease*

Please do not misunderstand me. A preacher, if he is faithful to his task, will sometimes make his hearers—and himself—uncomfortable. But that discomfort will arise from the stimulation of the conscience and not from the irritation of the nervous system, which has been communicated from the nerves of the preacher.

Some nervousness before preaching is natural and even desirable. When a preacher can boast that he 'has no nerves' and can 'take it in his stride', it is time he stopped preaching. That blatant attitude is not due to complete and humble confidence in the sufficiency of God, but to self-conceit. Further, it means that the man has lost the sense of the seriousness of his vocation. No man who realises that he is about to speak 'as a dying man to dying men' can be so cocksure.

A preacher in his mature years ought not to suffer from the kind of nervousness which may have afflicted him as a beginner —the fear that he would dry up, that he would not be able to get the words out, or that some other embarrassing evil would befall him. That is only the kind of anxiety which comes from doing something to which one is unaccustomed, and it may beset even an experienced person in an unfamiliar or unexpected situation. I once sat at a luncheon next to one of the most distinguished actresses of her time, who was due to respond to a toast at the end of the meal. She had written out her brief speech in enormous characters and surreptitiously under cover of the table-cloth she conned it again and again. She became so nervous that I wondered whether she would be able to speak at all. She did—but she, who could commit a whole play to memory and be word-perfect on the stage in front of packed houses, broke down in four lines of 'The Walrus and the Carpenter' through sheer fright before a comparative handful of people. She had probably been just as near to panic in her first stage appearances. I badly wanted to know, but I had not the courage to ask her! Part of the cure for this kind of nervousness is to take every opportunity to do the thing of which one is afraid. Bernard Shaw as a young man suffered terribly from 'nerves'. He would rise to speak shaking with nerves and pitifully self-conscious. Then he resolved that he would never miss a meeting or an opportunity to speak no matter how much he might suffer in the process. He kept this resolution, suffering agonies before his turn came, and wondering whether anyone could hear the painful hammering of his heart. He was so nervous that he could not read his notes, so apprehensive that he could not remember them, and he assumed that everyone realised his condition. But so determined was he to conquer his nervousness that he took every opportunity to speak, likening himself to 'an officer afflicted with cowardice, who takes every opportunity of going under fire to get over it and learn his business'.* The preacher must not show less courage and determination in overcoming nervousness. He must also try to overcome his fear of failure by remembering that he is not in the pulpit to enhance his own reputation or to give a brilliant performance. He is there to be used by God, or he ought not to be there at all, and if he does his best he can leave the rest to God's care. Some preachers torture themselves by being perfectionists. They are brought up in strictly religious homes by over-exacting parents, and, as long ago in childhood, now they are filled with anxiety and foreboding even when they know they have done their utmost. They always feel themselves to be working under 'the stern taskmaster's eye', and they will never be freed from their anxiety unless they can lay hold of the fact that God is more reasonable than their parents were.

Excessive nervousness, whatever its source, may make a congregation nervous unless it is well concealed. Especially if the preacher is young, or if he is a personality who spontaneously inspires affection, the people in the pews may be anxious on his behalf. If they are not in sympathy with him, their nervousness will be mingled with impatience because the man 'dithers' and is not 'on top of his job'.

There is, however, in some preachers a kind of tension which is not due to inexperience or fear of failure, but which has its roots deep within the personality. This causes the man's whole body to be taut, and leads him to emphasise even the most unimportant words so that after a time few people can stand the strain of listening to him. Moreover, in a crowd many things are infectious—like the cough which spreads all round the church or the clearing of throats if the preacher becomes husky. In the same way, the actual tension in the preacher's body will convey itself to some at least of his hearers. I know a woman who, on listening to a preacher of this kind for the first time, became so tense that she felt herself growing rigid and could only with

* Hesketh Pearson, *Bernard Shaw*, pp. 67 f.

difficulty restrain herself from rushing in panic through the door. This kind of tension may require psychological help in order to resolve hidden conflicts, but the preacher may be able to help himself and his congregation to be at ease by practising physical relaxation. We need not enter into the question as to whether emotions cause bodily states or bodily states produce emotions. Experience teaches us that the two are closely bound up together. An emotion grows by its bodily expression and can be reduced if its physical manifestations are controlled. Fear can be reduced if the breathing is slowed up by an effort of the will and the knees are braced to prevent them from knocking together. In the same way the over-tense preacher may be able to bring relief to himself and his congregation if he takes thought in the pulpit and deliberately relaxes his nerves and muscles. He is, of course, more likely to succeed in doing this if he practises the art of relaxation at other times.

(4) *The preacher must gain the attention of his congregation*

Forgive me saying a thing so obvious. I mean that he must gain it at once or he may not gain it at all. For this reason the beginning of a sermon is of supreme importance; it is even more important than the end. If people have not been made to listen at the beginning, it is unlikely that they will be doing so twenty minutes or half-an-hour later. It is sometimes said that a preacher should plunge straight into his subject. His business is so urgent that he has no time to waste. That principle may be sound enough when one is dealing with a specialised audience of people trained to listen and assembled with the sole and deliberate purpose of hearing a weighty utterance on a subject in which they are interested and on which they are already informed. Nobody would contend that a typical congregation is such an audience. It is made up of a mixed company of people—mixed in every way. They have come in different states of mind. Some are tired, some are distracted, some are not keen to hear what the preacher has to say, some—the adolescents at the back of the gallery?—are intending to devote the sermon time to more important concerns. Many of these people are not going to pay attention unless they can be made to feel at once, against all probabilities, that what the preacher is going to say is likely to be at least as interesting as their own thoughts. So, as a general rule, an introduction of some kind there must be, though it may be brief and to the point, and will be all the better if it is.

I cannot, myself, get on with the detailed preparation of a sermon until I have an opening which interests me, and which I may therefore hope will capture the attention of the congregation. I cannot prepare the 'body' of the sermon and trust that a serviceable opening will turn up before Sunday. When I have thought of a beginning which kindles a spark in me, I may go over it in my mind several times trying to get the 'feeling' of the congregation. If I do not feel them responding to it I cannot go on. I must think again. If I can feel them warming to it (I may, of course, be wrong in the event!) I can warm up myself and go ahead with the sermon.

There are many kinds of introduction, but the best will nearly always be those which make contact at some point with life as the people know and understand it. Few are prepared at once to be interested in the geography of the Holy Land or the doings of a remote King of Israel of whom they have never heard. Even a story from the *Gospels* or *The Acts of the Apostles* will not grip them unless it is approached by some road which started from their own experience or at least from the world in which they live and the contemporary situation with which they have to do. Sometimes an anecdote will help, but it must be relevant. We have no business to throw out a story, humorous or otherwise, like the opening gambit of an after-dinner speaker, even if it happens to be a good one. In any case, unless the theme immediately and naturally links on to it, any interest aroused will at once be lost. A bit of personal experience, a saying overheard, an item from the news, almost anything may provide the starting-point. Fiction, and more frequently biography, are happy hunting grounds.

Let us take one example. The autobiography of Lord Inman (better known to many as Philip Inman, the House Governor of Charing Cross Hospital) supplies an excellent opening for a sermon. He was the youngest of a family of four brothers. The father died when Philip was a small boy, and his mother was left to bring up the family with pitifully meagre resources. But she was a woman of indomitable courage and simple faith, and she was entirely devoid of self-pity. She began to take in washing—piles and piles of it. When a caretaker was required at a local school she took on the job, and when somebody was wanted to scrub the tombstones in the local churchyard at two shillings each she added that to her labours. At night, when the washing and the cleaning were done, she would work in the churchyard with one of the boys holding a lantern, and when the day was over she would often say, 'We will have a chapter before we go to bed.' Then the old family Bible was brought down from the shelf. There were many chapters which she specially liked, but one above all was her favourite. It was *Psalm* 103: 'Bless the Lord, O my soul: and all that is within me, bless his holy name. Bless the Lord, O my soul, and forget not all his benefits. . . .' 'I puzzled a great deal about this Psalm,' says Inman, 'and why Mother liked it so much. One night I asked her what *were* the benefits we had not to forget? A light came into her tired eyes and lit up her face. She answered, "I have my health and strength. We have a roof over our heads. And I have you, my children." '

That is a bit of life—real life. It is full of the pathos and heroism of everyday living. It touches emotions without being sentimental. It is the kind of thing that grips, and the sermon, no matter what may be the precise line of development, will grow naturally from it. It is also worth noting that this illustration will lead up to the text, and a text is sometimes more telling if it is not given in a bald announcement at the start of the sermon. In this case a great deal of its power would have been lost if the text had been announced first, and if this opening is handled well, attention has already been won before the text is revealed.

Sometimes the straightforward announcement of the title of the sermon makes a good point of departure, especially if the congregation is, on the whole, above average intelligence. But it must be an arresting title and one which conveys what the sermon will be about—not one of those fancy captions which ingenious or sensational preachers like to put on church notice-boards to bemuse passers-by. I remember how impressive it often was when Dr W. E. Orchard, in his great days at the King's Weigh House, used to look straight into the eyes of his congregation and say boldly, 'The subject of the sermon is . . .' The title always meant something, and, what is more, the sermon was on it! A question to be answered, a dilemma to be resolved, a statement to be challenged—the kinds of opening are legion.

The congregation should be given ample time to settle down and get over their preliminary shuffles and coughs. The moment when a congregation becomes completely quiet before the first word is spoken can be very impressive, but many preachers never allow time for it. A moment or two of silent recollection followed by a brief prayer or ascription is helpful. Then the introduction should begin in a quiet, but not inaudible, voice, and in a conversational manner. If the preacher opens loudly, vehemently or emotionally, the congregation will recoil. They are not yet attuned to this kind of thing, and may feel that the man in the pulpit is making himself rather ridiculous and that there is something forced and artificial about it all. They must be allowed time to warm up, and any attempt to capture attention by force will certainly prove futile.

(5) *The preacher must hold the attention of the congregation*

Obvious again, yet how often we fail to do it! And let us be under no delusions. The preacher has to hold it. People attend to a thing voluntarily only while they are so interested that they cannot 'take their minds off it'. Otherwise they 'have to make themselves listen', and most people are not prepared to exercise the will very much in this matter unless they can see a good reason for the effort. And when it comes to listening to sermons, most people can't. Nothing seems to hang on it. They won't have to pass an examination on the subject-matter. And let us be fair—for the great majority sustained attention over a long period is difficult. Before we complain too bitterly about the inattention of congregations, we may recall the devices to which we resorted as students to while away the weary hours as uninspiring lecturers droned on and on. The resources for profit or amusement of the pew are less than those of the classroom! We did not have a very bad conscience. We felt that if the lecturer could not make us listen he did not deserve our attention. So we cannot complain about the injustice of life if the congregation feels that the onus is upon the preacher.

The cardinal rule, then, is that the preacher must be interesting. The sad fact is that often he is not. Sir Leslie Stephen said that eighteenth-century sermons fell into three categories—dull, duller, dullest. If there has been a change for the better those labels cannot, unfortunately, be forthwith consigned to the waste-paper basket.

A congregation will not be interested unless the preacher himself is interested in what he is saying. It is said that an old Duke of Devonshire so bored himself by his speech in the House of Lords that he yawned in the middle of it. I have never actually seen a preacher do that, but I have seen some so lacking in animation that I have felt it might happen at any moment, and the congregation has not waited for a lead from the pulpit. I do not know who invented the phrase 'the sin of dullness', but in the pulpit it is a sin because it frustrates God's purpose and stands between Him and the people whom He is trying to reach through the preacher. 'How many sleep under us', said Richard Baxter, 'because our hearts and tongues are sleepy, and we bring not with us so much skill and zeal as to awake them.'

Monotony in all its forms is, of course, the chief enemy of attention. You cannot concentrate long on a thing that does not change or that you do not expect to change. If, by an effort of the will, you succeed in doing it, you may end by putting yourself into an hypnotic sleep! And there are so many varieties of monotony open to the preacher. His voice may be monotonous. He may speak almost in a monotone, or with the same inflexions recurring in every sentence, his voice rising and falling interminably to the same notes, and producing a dreadful singsong if the interval is great enough. There can also be monotony of speed, volume or emphasis, of gesture or immobility. It is said that a famous Scottish divine, who was quite motionless in the pulpit, was told that his delivery would be more interesting if he could introduce a few gestures. Being a humble man he took the advice and acted on it without delay. At the very beginning of his next sermon he raised one hand—and forgot to take it down until he had finished!

Dullness is a sin in the pulpit because it is avoidable. There is no need for monotony either in the matter of the sermon or its delivery. Voices differ naturally in tone and quality, but almost any man can learn, with help if his own ear is defective, to use a reasonable range, and to vary speed and emphasis. It may be unwise for a man who does not spontaneously use his hands in speaking to attempt to cultivate gestures. The result may be self-conscious and artificial, but anyone can experiment and seek the verdict of a candid friend. Certainly anyone can overcome the kind of immobility which gives the impression that a statue has somehow contrived to speak.

Dullness of language and expression can also be overcome. Sentences of uniform length, all well-rounded and perfectly polished, can grow monotonous. Speech needs also sharp, crisp sentences, and sometimes the phrase which jolts the somnolent mind. According to Bernard Shaw, if a man does not say things in a provocative way he may as well not say them at all, for nobody will pay any attention. There is truth in this, but without reservation it is a dangerous doctrine. There are preachers who take delight in being provocative. They obviously enjoy it so much and think themselves so clever and daring that the congregation

is annoyed by their naïve attempt to shock, and is not stimulated
to think about the truth of what has been said. As for the preacher
himself, he has never grown up; he has not left behind the
adolescent who tries to outrage his elders with rude words and
heroic poses.

(6) *The preacher must make every member of the congregation feel
that he is being addressed personally*

Queen Victoria used to complain that Mr Gladstone talked to her
as though she were a public meeting. A congregation must never
be addressed even in the mass as if it were a public meeting.
Indeed, it must never be treated as a 'mass' at all, for, as we have
seen, preaching is the most intimate and personal of all forms of
public speech. The aim of it is to bring about an encounter
between the individual soul and God, and therefore the preacher
must try to make every one of his hearers feel that he is being
spoken to particularly and personally.

If this is to be achieved, the method of delivery is important.
Broadly speaking, there are three ways: a sermon may be read, or
memorised, or preached extempore with or without the aid of
notes. The advantages and disadvantages of them all have been
considered again and again in lectures and books on preaching,
but we must look at them once more from the standpoint of the
art of communication. It cannot be said that any of them is right
or wrong. They have all been successful in the hands of masters.

(*a*) *Reading.* Some people have a rooted prejudice against the
reading of a sermon. They will not admit that it is real preaching
at all. In *The Little Minister* Sir James Barrie says, 'The old
minister would rather have remained to die in his pulpit than
surrender it to one who read his sermons. Others may blame him
for this, but I must say here plainly that I never hear a minister
reading without wishing to send him back to college.' As a
sweeping judgement that is grossly unfair. He would have had
to send Dr Jowett and Dr J. D. Jones back to college along with

many other famous preachers, ancient and modern. Dr Jones was one of the most fluent extempore speakers of his time, but he always read his sermons. Yet he read them so well that very few of his hearers ever realised how closely he was adhering to his manuscript. The advantage of the method, supposing the sermon to be well written, is that it makes for conciseness of expression, exactness of phrasing and compactness of argument, and eliminates the danger of the meanderings which can destroy the effectiveness of a sermon.

But it has the obvious disadvantage that unless it is read so well that nobody is conscious that it is being read, the manuscript gets between the preacher and the congregation. In a witty passage of his *Lectures To My Students*, Spurgeon likens the head movements of a preacher reading to those of a hen drinking! A little extreme, perhaps, but in some ways a recognisable likeness! Even when the reading is much better done, the obvious lowering of eyes to a manuscript breaks continuity and destroys the impression that the preacher is engaged in personal conversation with the hearer. In conversations you do not refer to notes to see what is coming next. Moreover, some preachers who are free enough to look at their congregations for a much longer time than a hen lifts her head are apt to lower their eyes and concentrate entirely on the reading desk when they come to a particularly important passage and want to be sure of getting it quite right. This may also be a fault in a man who preaches from more or less full notes. But it is precisely then that the preacher should look straight at the people. If a preacher decides that for him there is no alternative to reading, he should spare no pains to create the pardonable illusion that he is not reading.

(*b*) *Memorising*. This method was favoured by many distinguished preachers of the past and was formerly used much more than it is today. Among them was John Angell James of Carrs Lane. In 1819 he preached the Annual Sermon for the London Missionary Society in the old Surrey Chapel. This is part of the account of it given by his colleague and successor, Dr R. W. Dale: 'The Sermon, which occupies fifty pages of the Collected Works, and lasted two hours, was not read, but delivered *memoriter*. The preacher's brother sat in the pulpit with the manuscript in his hand, prepared, if there was a moment's hesitation, to suggest the forgotten word; but from first to last the discourse was delivered exactly as it stood on the paper—not an epithet or a preposition was changed. At the close of the first hour, the preacher requested permission to pause for a few minutes, and the people sang a hymn. Such was the excitement of the congregation, that during this temporary interruption of the discourse, oranges were thrown into the pulpit to refresh the exhausted orator. This hymn finished, he rose again, and recovering his strength, thundered on for another hour. . . .'*

This description of a *tour de force* indicates the one merit which memorising shares with reading—'the discourse was delivered exactly as it stood on the paper'. It has the advantage over reading that it leaves the eyes perfectly free for contact with the congregation. I cannot think there is much else to be said in its favour.

It puts an immense labour on the preacher unless he has a memory like that of a former British Prime Minister, Mr Bonar Law, who, when he had thought out a problem, 'would dictate his speech to his secretary, read it over once for accuracy, and never look at it again before delivering it. He had no need even to refer to a note, but he practised an effective oratorical trick in debate or during an address of taking a little note-book from his pocket and apparently consulting it before announcing a set of figures. There was no entry at all in the book.'† Angell James, too, must have had a prodigious memory, especially as there was an immense piling up of epithets.

A more serious objection is that it is very difficult to deliver a memorised speech naturally. That, perhaps, did not apply so much in the old days, when declamation was the fashion, as it

* R. W. Dale: *The Life and Letters of J. A. J.*, p. 102.
† Frank Owen: *Tempestuous Journey*, p. 223.

would now when a more conversational style is 'called for. A speaker using this method is in much the same position as an actor, except that he himself has composed the speech. Only a very accomplished actor can make a rehearsed speech sound like real conversation. A second-rate one will almost certainly over-emphasise unimportant bits, will be too precise with his punctuation, will get some of his inflexions wrong, and in short will rob the words of much of their spontaneity and life.

Again, the memoriser, if he is adroit in the use of the method, may appear to be free, but he is not so in reality. He is not able to respond to the congregation beyond any modification in the manner of his delivery, and that he has probably worked out beforehand. He must stick to his prepared script or he will be lost. He cannot change his matter or presentation in order to make his message more effective as he senses the mood or need of his hearers. And—most alarming prospect—there is always the moment when he will forget his words entirely and, unless he has an obliging brother at hand to prompt him, there will be no help nigh!

(c) *Extempore.* Extempore preaching does not, of course, mean that the sermon is improvised. The method, as we shall see, calls for as much preparation as either of the others, and in some respects for more. A sermon which is to be preached extempore may in fact be written out in full, but in delivery the preacher makes no attempt to reproduce the language of his manuscript. Inevitably, if he is familiar with the written sermon, he will, without trying to do so, use some of its expressions. But he does not *depend* upon doing so. It is not the language but the ideas that he is concerned to reproduce, and he will clothe them in the words that come to him at the moment of delivery.

It is generally supposed that extempore preaching is the most difficult kind. It is probably difficult to the point of impossibility for some men, but I am convinced that it is within the capacity of many who have never attempted it. What are the requirements?

(i) Some facility in the use of words; the ability to clothe thoughts in a suitable form of expressioh. This does not mean eloquence. Too great a fluency may be a positive hindrance, because the preacher may be tempted to a verbosity which would have been severely pruned in a written sermon.

(ii) Some memory—but not necessarily a good one. As we have noticed, the preacher does not memorise paragraphs, but only words and brief phrases which bring ideas to his mind. Reliance on memory can be still further reduced by the use of a few brief notes containing headings. These require no more than a glance and will not curtail freedom. A preacher who does not normally need even these brief reminders is extremely foolish if he has not such an aid somewhere within reach. The most experienced preacher, because he is tired, or not so well prepared as he ought to be, or because he is distracted by some happening in the congregation, may suddenly find his mind a complete blank and be unable to recover himself. That is a desperate situation in which every extempore speaker finds himself at least once in a lifetime! In point of fact, he may much more often than once in a lifetime find himself momentarily at a loss. The thread is broken; he cannot remember the next point. But he is not in the plight of the memoriser who breaks down. Indeed, his situation is not serious at all unless he panics. If he pauses a moment or two longer than he would choose, the congregation will not notice anything amiss, although it may seem an age to him. He can play for time by repeating in slightly different words what he has just said, or by summing up the point he has made if he has reached the end of a section. So long as he keeps calm he can do this with a little bit of his mind. The rest of it is free to recover the missing idea—and it generally will. He can fortify himself with the thought that every extempore preacher has found himself in this predicament and has emerged safely. I once saw a famous Scottish preacher, who would have scorned the use of notes, lost in this way. For the moment he could not for the life of him recall his next point. So he cruised round in a little circle, picked up his bearings and sailed happily on. Probably no one in the congregation sensed his momentary peril or detected the manœuvre by which he extricated himself except a few preachers who, in similar distress, had more than once employed it themselves!

(iii) *Thorough preparation.* This is the essential condition of good extemporary preaching. It is this which reduces to a minimum the role of memory. If a sermon is disorderly there is no hope of producing it in the pulpit unless every idea of the hotch-potch has been committed independently to memory. If the sermon is well constructed, with one idea following another in close and logical sequence, it will unroll itself like a ball of thread in which there are no tangles. The law of association gets to work.

I sometimes hold a kind of post-mortem on a sermon I have preached. It is a salutary discipline. I compare what I believe I did say with what I had intended to say. If something fell out of the sermon in delivery I almost always find that it was something which should never have been in it at all. It was an idea which had no real relevance, no place in the logical progression, or it was an illustration which had been dragged in because I liked it and not because it really illustrated. It was something stuck on, a mere accretion which was no part of the organic whole. So, mercifully, it dropped off before it could do any harm.

(iv) *Courage to take the plunge.* I am sure many more ministers could win the freedom of extempore preaching if only they would put their manuscripts aside and make the attempt. It is never too late to begin. A few years ago I met an old minister whom I had known for years as a most painstaking preacher, who wrote out every word of every sermon in a neat and careful hand. Now, at four-score years, he had lost his sight. 'Can't see to read now,' he said without a trace of self-pity, 'so I have to preach extempore. And', he added gleefully, 'they tell me I'm preaching better than ever I did.' I have no doubt he was—and he deserved to be!

(7) *The preacher must be clear*

I do not have opportunities to hear many sermons and therefore am not in a good position to judge, but I suspect that a great weakness of much modern preaching is a lack of clarity. I am confirmed in that impression by the kind of comment that is often made by people in the pews: 'We didn't know what he was talking about,' or 'We couldn't see what he was getting at.' Such comments generally refer not to a high-brow (American = 'egg-head') or a learned professor who has made the mistake of preaching over the heads of the congregation, but to a man who would not be capable of profound academic discussions or flights into the rarefied atmosphere of philosophic speculation. He is an ordinary, average minister, as most of us are, who could be a good and helpful preacher if only he were not so muddled that his congregation is never sure whence he comes or whither he goes, and suspects that he is not either.

If a preacher is ever to be clear to his congregation he must first be clear to himself. He must know exactly what his sermon is to be about and what he intends it to do. Before ever he sets pen to paper he must crystallise his purpose in a word, a phrase, a sentence, a question to be answered. He must also have a clear plan of the route to his destination, and he must keep to it whatever may be the temptation to wander down seductive by-ways. To change the figure—since a sermon is more often likened to a building than a journey—he must have a design for the structure. The question now is: at what point in preparation is the plan to be made?

Some preachers would say that the drawing up of the plan is the first piece of work to be done, but in his *Nine Lectures on Preaching* Dr Dale insists that this is not the proper order. 'Some preachers', he says, 'begin with their "plan". They think that it is their business to "divide" their subject or their text; and having constructed their divisions they fill them up as best they can. . . . But it is my impression that the habit of making the "plan" of the sermon first and getting the materials afterwards is likely to have an injurious effect on a man's preaching. The "plan" of the sermon is the order in which the materials are arranged, and it seems to me that the reasonable method is to arrange the materials when you have got them to arrange—not before.'* Most subsequent writers have agreed that the first business is to collect materials, and that the preacher, having settled his text or theme and the object of his sermon, should then write down any relevant ideas that occur to him just as they come, arranging them afterwards in whatever order will give the most effective presentation. This is, of course, sound advice, though I must confess that I do not always follow it. I frequently find that when I have defined its purpose, the 'plan' of the sermon will present itself as a whole almost in a flash, it may be while I am shaving or drying the dishes! Perhaps, however, its emergence is not always so sudden as it seems. I am a great believer in the subconscious incubation of sermons.†

One thing is certain. Whenever it is made, a plan there must be before the final preparation is begun. But there need be no invariable form for it. It used to be the custom for preachers to construct their sermons on the three-decker principle—three 'points' with an introduction and a conclusion. But there is nothing sacrosanct about the number three and the constant adherence to it would make for monotony. The only valid rule surely is that every sermon shall have the number of 'points' necessary for the proclamation of the message and the achievement of its purpose—no less, and certainly no more. There may be two or half a dozen. Not long ago I heard a preacher with an international reputation set nine points before his hearers. He expounded each one clearly and tersely, but not many listeners could absorb so much at a single sitting.

The preacher must constantly examine and criticise his sermons from the standpoint of clarity. As he goes over his work in his

---

* R. W. Dale: *Nine Lectures on Preaching*, pp. 136 f.
† cf. Iremonger's biography of William Temple.

study he must cultivate the kind of imagination which enables him to put himself alongside the ordinary listeners in the pews so that he can hear as they will hear, having no specialised knowledge and no foreknowledge of what the preacher intends to achieve by the sermon or where it is expected to lead. We were fortunate to have as the City Organist of Birmingham for many years that great musician, Dr G. D. Cunningham. Organ music, as you know, can be a terrible jumble of sounds in which it is quite impossible to distinguish anything. Cunningham's playing was never like that. There was an unrivalled crispness and clarity about it. I once asked him how he did it. 'Oh,' he said, 'I think I can tell you that. I listen as I play, and if *I* can't hear it clearly I don't expect my audience will. So I try again.' Soon afterwards I heard an interesting commentary on that. A church organist told me that during the war he worked in the Food Office which for a time was in the basement of the Town Hall. 'G. D.' used to practise overhead for his weekly recitals. 'As an organist of sorts', said my friend, 'I revelled in it, but sometimes he nearly drove us crazy. One day he was dissatisfied with his playing of a few bars. He went over them sixty-six times in succession. I counted!' It would lift the level of preaching beyond all telling if ministers would take as much trouble to make clear the message of God as Cunningham did to make clear the message of the great composers.

Besides the construction of a suitable plan, clarity depends upon at least four other factors:

(a) *Simplicity.* Firstly, simplicity of thought. Some men can make even the most straightforward thing seem complex. Others can make difficult things understandable to ordinary minds. These are the men who have so mastered their subject that they are capable of reducing it to its simplest terms. When a preacher is incomprehensible to his congregation it is not generally because his thought is too profound for them, but because he himself has not worked his way right into and through his subject. That does not mean, of course, that there are no mysteries and no insoluble problems in religion and life. There are many, and the preacher must sometimes tell his congregation that they must not expect the short and easy answer, or, indeed, any complete answer at all. But some men, because of the fog in their own minds, can create confusion where there need be none.

Secondly, there must be simplicity of language. Anything that is worth saying can be said in familiar words and generally in short words. And let us shun jargon like the plague—jargon of all kinds. It is sometimes necessary when we are dealing with personal problems in the pulpit to impart some of the insights which modern psychology has given us, but there is no need to lard our speech with terms from the textbooks. If we understand what we are talking about we can say it just as well in everyday language. And the jargon of the theological classroom is an equal menace. It is necessary sometimes to use the great words of the New Testament, words like 'justification', 'sanctification' and 'redemption', but we must remember that they are unfamiliar words to most people in the pews, and we must make sure that they are understood. We should be exasperated if we went to a lecture by a scientific expert in the congregation who used terms familiar to himself and his kind but would not bother to explain them to laymen like us.

(b) *Concreteness.* Few people without academically trained minds are capable of really abstract thought—and many even of them are not! The vast majority think in terms of everyday life and practical duties. Philosophical discussion of moral problems will get them nowhere. In this respect, as in others, Jesus is the preacher's model. He is always 'down to earth', and talking about real situations. When we speak of the meaning of Christian life we must give simple, detailed examples which translate principles into terms of daily life in home and street, office and factory, school and hospital.

(c) *The avoidance of everything irrelevant*

If our plan is properly constructed there will be no place for things which are no integral part of the design but are merely stuck on by way of ornament, like bits and pieces adhering to Victorian furniture and buildings. The Victorians were given to decorating their sermons in the same way. Dale says of Angell James's sermon, to which I have referred, 'The thought is sometimes crushed by a mass of glittering ornament.' The elementary principle of design is 'fitness for purpose', and there is beauty as well as utility in good, clean lines, whether in a piece of furniture, a building or a sermon. Illustrations, quotations, 'purple patches', which are merely stuck on, destroy the clarity of design and cannot too soon be knocked off.

The same can be said of irrelevant arguments and facts, however interesting and useful they might be in another context. A preacher must stick to the point. Some years ago I met a Scottish engineer who had been a student under Lord Kelvin. In his opinion Kelvin was not a good lecturer, though he would go to endless trouble to clear up a student's difficulties by personal tuition. In class he would often set out to elucidate a problem on the blackboard, but leaving his original purpose far behind he would cover the board with masses of figures while his bewildered students amused themselves as best they could. Unlike some teachers, however, Kelvin was aware of his weakness and adopted drastic measures to deal with it. He fixed up a 'buzzer' which went off at ten-minute intervals. When it startled Kelvin out of his abstractions he would put out his hand to stop it, saying, 'I am sorry, gentlemen. I have been wandering.' The buzzer technique might help in some pulpits, but if it is to achieve perfection we shall need a new Lord Kelvin who will devise an instrument capable of detecting automatically when a preacher is wandering and buzzing him down immediately, for, unlike Lord Kelvin, some preachers do not appear to know when they are wandering or even that they are addicted to it at all.

(d) *Illustration*. I include what I have to say about illustrations
under the head of clarity for the obvious reason that illustrations
are intended to clarify. They are meant to throw light on truth
so that it can be more plainly seen. They also aim at making it
seen in such a vivid way that it cannot be forgotten, and in this a
good illustration often succeeds so well that, as every preacher
knows, it will be remembered when the rest of the sermon has
passed into oblivion. It may be, of course, that a hearer will long
afterward recall a story without remembering the point of it. In
that case, although it may have been a striking story in itself, it
was probably not a good illustration. The illustrations of Jesus
are so apt that nobody would ever have recalled one of His
stories or little sketches of everyday life drawn with a few bold
strokes without at once bringing to mind the truth about God or
life that it was designed to teach.

Most of the illustrations used by Jesus are drawn from life—
the life familiar to the ordinary people who heard Him speak.
The preacher who is observant and sympathetic, as Jesus was,
will have no difficulty in finding illustrations all around him. He
also has a much wider field to draw upon, because in the twentieth
century the world is brought to him by newspaper and radio.
Moreover, without being a scientist or doctor he will find a great
deal of useful material in science and medicine. He will not be
able to read weighty textbooks on these subjects, but there are
works by authoritative writers which give in a popular way many
of the results of modern research. When he is not using a written
source but is relying on impressions or memory, he will be wise
to check up with a scientific or medical friend. As I have already
confessed, I have learned from my own errors that it is better not
to cull illustrations from unfamiliar fields unless we can be sure
of accuracy. Travel books and biographies also yield stores of
material, and in the matter of biography the Bible is, of course, a
library in itself. Good illustrations may, indeed, come from
almost anywhere except the encyclopaedia of quotations or the
book of 'quotable anecdotes'. It is possible that these first-aid

outfits for lazy preachers may occasionally provide something useful, but there is none of the satisfaction which a preacher feels as a craftsman when he takes an illustration that he has made or discovered for himself and fits it exactly into place in his sermon.

Let us note three things by way of warning:

(i) *We must not claim as our own experiences which are actually second-hand.* Some preachers might be prepared to defend the practice of speaking in the first person on the ground that it makes for vividness and conviction. It seems to me dishonest, and it is certainly dangerous. Any preacher who is addicted to it will be lucky if he is not caught out sooner or later. A deacon once told me that his minister had begun a story by saying, 'When I was travelling in the train to London last week . . .', and then had proceeded to relate something which had happened to *him*. 'But', said the deacon, 'it didn't happen to him. I read it last week in the same magazine. It has shaken my faith in him. I can never be quite sure any more that he is telling the truth.' Even a bishop can err in this matter. It was reported in a newspaper that at a school prize-giving a certain dignitary had said, 'When I was a young curate in X . . .', and that he had gone on to tell how he had been sent by his vicar to the station to meet a clergyman whom he did not know. Accosting a likely-looking man, who was not wearing a clerical collar, he asked him if he was the Rev Mr B., and received the reply, 'No, it is my indigestion that makes me look like this!' Now there can scarcely be a more venerable 'chestnut' in the whole range of 'funny' stories. Of course, it could have happened that the man, never having heard the story, really did hit upon this reply by sheer coincidence. After all, we are told if an infinite number of monkeys tapped the keys of typewriters for an infinite time they would produce all the plays of Shakespeare! Or the man might have heard the story and thought he could fire this bit of repartee at the curate who might be too young to know it. Whatever the schoolgirls thought, none of the adults present, who had been familiar with the story for years—

and they must have been about 99 per cent.—believed that the bishop was telling the truth when he said the incident happened to him.

(ii) *Illustrations must sound authentic.* Preaching some time ago at a college in an ancient university city, I described an incident which happened in the Old Vic theatre. In brief it was this: at a performance of *King Lear* a man sitting in a seat in front of me was so completely absorbed in the play that it ceased to be a play for him and became real life, so that when Lear was wandering on the moor in the raging storm, and the 'effects' made us hear the wind howling and the rain pelting down, he unconsciously shuddered and turned up his coat collar. After the service a don told me that he liked my illustrations. 'But', he said, 'you couldn't get away with that one about the Old Vic. You had so obviously cooked it up.' I said I only wished I had the imagination to invent such a story and, being a good friend of mine, he accepted my assurance that it really had happened. I shall probably continue to use the story from time to time because I believe that in its context it is a good illustration, and nobody had ever—overtly!—queried it before. But for my friend it was not helpful because it distracted him. He was more interested in speculating on whether it could have happened and in deciding that it couldn't than in its point as an illustration. Although, as I have said, I do not propose to discard the anecdote, I find in my friend's scepticism a warning that it is unwise to use illustrations which seem wildly improbable. Those which are given as creations of the imagination and which are accepted as such are, of course, in another category. Truth is stranger than fiction, but when we narrate what verges on the incredible it is well to give the source or some other guarantee of its authenticity.

(iii) *Pastoral confidences must not be betrayed.* Pastoral work will provide some of our most effective illustrations because they are from real life and often life at its most heroic or tragic. As an example let me quote the use made of pastoral experience by Dr Herbert Gray. I take it from his book *Finding God*, but I am sure he must have used these incidents in sermons, perhaps, as I like to think, at Carrs Lane, where he was associate preacher for some years. He is speaking of the way to God through suffering: 'Thirty years ago I asked an old man in London whether he would care to live his life over again on condition that it would turn out exactly the same life as he had lived. I was prepared to hear a fervent "God forbid", because that is what many would say. But after thinking for a while the man replied deliberately, "Yes, and especially would I like to live again through my times of trouble." Being young and inexperienced, I asked, in great astonishment, "But why?" To which he replied, "Because it was in these times that I learned most about God!" I took my question a little later to two sensitive cultivated women who were my friends, and they, after thinking said, "Yes, and especially the time when our sister was so ill." Once again I asked why, and I got the answer, "Because it was in that awful time that we learnt what God can do for us." '*

Dr Gray was speaking after the lapse of thirty years when those to whom he referred were dead, and nobody would be able to identify them. In this case it might not have mattered much if they had been identified except in so far as they might have been embarrassed, but the situation is otherwise when the illustration concerns intimate personal relationships or someone's temptations, follies or sins. In these cases identification might be disastrous, and, moreover, if people feel that they may be dissected or held up as specimens in the pulpit, they will certainly not give the minister a chance to know the inside of their lives and so his pastoral work will be crippled. Sometimes it may be possible on the basis of life situations to construct illustrations in which the circumstance as well as the actors are so completely changed that there can be no possible chance of recognition. Then it will have to be presented as an imaginary case, and will

* Herbert Gray: *Finding God*, p. 105.

be introduced with some such words as 'Imagine a situation like this . . .' Occasionally it may happen that in a pastoral interview somebody will make a remark which shows such deep insight that a preacher knows it would be of immense help to other people. Then he can ask permission to use it. 'You know, what you have just said would help a lot of people. Do you mind if some time I pass it on in a sermon? Of course, I won't give a clue as to who said it.' This is certain: whether or not a preacher is often able to use sayings and incidents that have emerged in his pastoral work, his preaching will be enlarged and deepened by all that comes to him as he seeks to help and comfort others, for he will be in touch with the real lives of real people.

(8) *The preacher must appeal to the whole man*

We have said that the aim of the preacher is to bring about a personal encounter between the individual soul and God, and, as a result of that encounter, a self-commitment to Him. Sometimes the sermon has the quite definite object of bringing about conversions, i.e. the initial act of self-commitment on the part of those who are living without God, so that they turn and face towards God instead of away from Him, and at that moment begin a new life of trust in Him. But every sermon, even one that is preached primarily to the already converted and consists largely of instruction, aims at self-commitment in some respect. If a Christian duty is expounded or a virtue elaborated, there is implicit or explicit—and it should generally be explicit—the call for decision and action.

If such commitment is to be brought about the appeal must be to the whole self. We recognise that there was something artificial about the tripartite division, beloved by the Faculty Psychologists, into intellect, feeling and will. Nor is conscience a separate and distinct function or 'organ' of personality. The thinking part of us does not work in a compartment of its own into which there is no leakage from the other division which houses the emotions. Emotion can be excluded from reason only by the most rigorous discipline, and never is the separation complete once we get outside the realms of pure science and mathematics. André Maurois quotes Pascal to the effect that if geometry stirred us emotionally as much as politics we would not be able to expound it so well. Not even scientists can always achieve detachment when expounding their own subject. There are certainly some psychologists, for example, who cannot think of Freud without emotional revulsion, and there are some Freudians who cannot think of other schools without passion or prejudice. There is no such reasoning faculty naturally distinct from the rest of the mind. As Professor Laura Stebbing observes, '*I* think, not *something* thinks in me. My intellect does not function apart from the rest of my personality.'* But remembering that we are dissecting something which can live and function only as a whole, we will for the moment divide personality into reason, emotion, conscience and will.

(*a*) *The appeal to reason*. There is no need to preach 'high-brow' sermons in order to appeal to reason. We have already made a plea for simplicity. But the preacher must present a sound case. His argument must be logical. It is not to be expected that everything can be established by pure reason, for reason is not the only way to truth either in religion or in other realms of life and thought. There must, however, be nothing illogical. It is not honest to try to gloss over a weak point in an argument, or to attempt by eloquence a cheap sneer at opponents, or any other trick, to pull wool over the eyes of the congregation. A preacher may be sure that some minds will be acute enough to detect the subterfuge and he will lose their respect, as he richly deserves.

There are two ways, I think, in which preachers are specially apt to do violence to logic. One is in the making of rash generalisations. We are inclined to make sweeping statements, especially about those who do not accept Christianity or those whose moral

* Laura Stebbing: *Thinking to some Purpose*, p. 32.

standards we attack. This is often due to excessive zeal or a desire to make people 'sit up and think', but the man in the pew has only to produce one instance which does not fit in, and he has exploded your generalisation and at the same time lost faith in your desire to be fair and honest. He will probably suspect that you do not feel that your case is sound, and that therefore you are not too scrupulous in the means you use to bolster it up. The other pitfall is the use of false or faulty analogies. Argument from analogy has been one of the favourite devices of prophets and preachers at least since the time of Nathan. Properly used it is legitimate, and it can be useful because it appeals to people who could not easily follow an abstract argument. Unfortunately it is often improperly used because the resemblances on which the analogy is based, even if there are many of them, are not in essentials, while the differences, though fewer, are more significant. As has often been pointed out, in analogies we must not count resemblances, we must *weigh* them.

The preacher must also remember that if he is to convince his hearers he will often have to repeat the point he is trying to drive home. He may, indeed, have to go over it several times if it is to be understood and remembered. Most of us find that when we have read a few pages of a book we sometimes have to turn back and read them again, especially if they contain close argument and our attention has flagged a little. The man in the pew whose thoughts have wandered—and perhaps he has not been entirely to blame!—or who is not quite so quick off the mark as some of his neighbours, may give up in despair if he feels he has lost the thread and cannot pick it up again. But it is not only those of a low intelligence quotient who will benefit by this repetition. 'The late Brandon Matthews of Columbia University, once told a class, all of whom had at least one college degree, that experience had taught him that he must expect to repeat a thing at least three times before such graduate students would grasp his meaning.'* But there is art in successful repetition. It is never

* Arleigh B. Williamson: *Speaking in Public*, pp. 262 f.

merely repetition. What is essentially the same idea must be repeated in a slightly varied form or with a difference of approach. And it must not be repeated in any form so often that it becomes boring, for in that case some of the listeners will say, 'This is where we came in', and, mentally at least, they will make for the exit.

The preacher, then, must seek to convince the reason, but he must respect the personality of his hearers too much ever to try to side-track it or overthrow it. Therefore he will be very careful in the use of suggestion. Canon Dewar says that etymologically the word 'means "to bring in from underneath", and that is what the word does. It brings into the mind an idea, or an emotion, or a desire, beneath the level of the critical judgement. In suggestion the critical reason is by-passed. Thus when an idea enters the mind by means of suggestion it evades being cross-questioned by the intellect. It is accepted without criticism.'* Canon Dewar points out, quite rightly, that many of the ideas which people hold have found entry into their minds in this way, and he seems prepared to defend the wholesale use of suggestion in preaching. The prestige of the speaker is, as he says, one factor making for the ready acceptance of suggestions, but it is not a good thing that ideas should be taken uncritically from a bishop, merely because he is a bishop, which would be rejected if they were offered by a humbly placed clergyman. No minister has any right to try to impress a congregation by his prestige. That would be to take a page out of the book of the dictators who, with all the apparatus of showmanship, exalt their prestige with such phenomenal success that they succeed in by-passing the critical reason of multitudes who are quite ready to have their thinking done for them. The only kind of suggestion which is legitimate—if it can properly be termed suggestion—is what Canon Dewar calls 'suggestion by imitation', which, he says, can happen only in one way: through the life of the preacher. 'If he is obviously a man of God, that fact has immense suggestive power, which will reinforce his sermons, and make up, to some extent at least,

* Canon Dewar: *Psychology and the Parish Priest*, p. 11.

for their technical deficiencies.' But the goodness of a preacher shining through his words and personality is surely not a suggestion designed to by-pass the critical reason, but rather a powerful argument for the truth of the Gospel he proclaims. The people said that Jesus taught as one having authority and not as the scribes. Beyond question the prestige of office and the trappings of authority enabled the scribes to get over by suggestion a great deal that would never have passed the critical reason if their hearers had been encouraged to use it. The personality of Jesus, what He so manifestly was, appealed to reason and authenticated His words.

It is true that many of the things which most people accept and believe are planted in their minds below the level of conscious reason by politicians, advertisers and publicists of all sorts. But the preacher cannot stoop to such uses of suggestion. Some of his hearers will have but a slender foundation in reason for what they believe. Their capacity for reasoning is small, and some are mentally lazy and will not use such powers as they have. But the preacher must not take advantage of this. He must constantly be trying to stab their minds awake and make them see that to love God with the mind means using to the full the reason He has given them.

If conscience compels the preacher to forgo the use of a means of winning adherents which is so potent in the hands of others, he may console himself by remembering that the effects of suggestion, though striking at first, are often of short duration. Psychotherapists formerly used suggestion a great deal as a method of cure, and it appeared to work miracles. But after a time it became evident that in many cases the patient was not cured at all. Suggestion had done no more than remove symptoms. The cause of the trouble had not been rooted out, and in due course other symptoms were produced. Dr R. H. Thouless points out that a more serious objection still was that 'the deep-seated cause of disease might even be made worse; the use of suggestion might strengthen those irrational and involuntary processes of

the patient's mind which were the cause of his mental disorders'.*
Here lies the explanation of the quick 'relapse of many converts
made at revival meetings, where suggestion is one of the main
methods employed. They have never been convinced, because
their reason has been by-passed. Symptoms have been removed
but no deep changes have been made. On the contrary, irrational
processes and uncontrolled emotions have been stirred up so that
the last state is worse than the first.

(b) *The appeal to emotion.* There are two reasons why there must
be an appeal to the emotions. First, emotion as well as reason is a
way to truth. This is especially so in the realm of personal
relationships. A man may discover some things about a woman
from facts that he has already observed and verified. That amount
of knowledge is open to anyone who is sufficiently interested to
acquire it. But there is a deeper knowledge of her personality
which is accessible to him only when he falls in love and finds a
like response in her. Religion is essentially a personal relationship
with God, and therefore there are whole ranges of spiritual truth
which can never be discovered and appropriated by cold reason
alone. They await a stirring and ultimate surrender of the
emotional life. It may well be that some of us are too afraid of
emotion in religion. There can be no true friendship without
emotion. At least there will be gratitude for what our friend is to
us, and perhaps for what he has done for us, and there will be
shame when we fail him. How can any man catch even a fleeting
vision of the purity, beauty and majesty of God without being
moved to reverence, which is 'love mingled with awe'? How can
it be borne in upon him that Christ died for him—which is inescapable on any theology of the Cross—without his being deeply
stirred to gratitude? How can he be brought face to face with his
own betrayals and selfishness without knowing the pangs of peni-
tence? The preacher has every right so to present his message that
he will appeal to the deepest emotions of his hearers, but if he has a

* R. H. Thouless: *Straight Thinking in War-time*, p. 70.

proper respect for his message, for the congregation and for himself he will scorn emotionalism which is merely superficial and does not touch the depths of personality. He will not seek to produce this state by his words, by a worked-up display of feeling in himself, by sentimental music or other doubtful aids. Some time ago I attended a great meeting addressed by a well-known evangelist. His sermon was surprisingly free of emotionalism, but after he had made his 'appeal' an enormous choir sang again and again a hymn obviously designed to work on the susceptibilities of the vast crowd while he continued to urge people to come forward. Time after time they sang it softly, almost crooningly. And it was effective enough. The people came, slowly at first and then in increasing numbers as the emotional tension heightened and suggestion worked more easily. But I suspect that some who came were resentful when the artificially induced emotion had worn off. They probably felt like people who had been drugged and induced to do something to which reason had never assented.

The second reason why the preacher must appeal to genuine and healthy emotion is that feeling is the spur to action. Adam Bede was speaking sound sense when he said, 'It isn't notions sets people doing the right things—it's feelings.' A man may know all the statistics about, say, refugees, and his reason may tell him that he ought to do what he can to help, but he probably will not act until something or somebody arouses his compassion. And the preacher is always out for action.

The emotions to which the preacher may appeal are, broadly speaking, fear and love.

In the past, and to a lesser extent in the present, certain types of evangelists and preachers have spared no pains to terrify their hearers with the threat of hell. Jonathan Edwards, an American preacher in the early eighteenth century, used considerable skill in building up a cumulative effect. Beginning by asking his congregation to imagine themselves 'cast into a fiery oven, or a great furnace, where their pain would be as much greater than that occasioned by accidentally touching a coal of fire, as the heat is greater', he would then invite them to imagine what it would be like if not a finger but the whole body 'full of quick sense' were to be in such a furnace for one minute—a quarter of an hour—twenty-four hours—a thousand years—millions and millions of ages, knowing that their torments would be no nearer to an end and that they 'never, never would be delivered'. It is not surprising to be told that 'the terror which gripped his audiences made them cry aloud for mercy so that the preacher sometimes could not be heard, and they grasped their benches to prevent themselves from slipping into the pit'. In the same school of preachers was an evangelist who told a New York congregation in 1907: 'I preach hell because God puts His special blessing on it, convicting sinners and sanctifying believers, arousing the Church to greater efforts for the salvation of the perishing. . . . *Hell has been running for six thousand years.* It is filling up every day. Where is it? About eighteen miles from here. *Which way is it? Straight down*—not over eighteen miles, down in the bowels of the earth.'*

All this is dreadful, but because we must eschew such crudities it does not follow that there is no proper place for an appeal to fear. There may be a hell, even if we cannot picture it as a fiery oven or a great furnace; there may be a judgement, even if it is not to be imagined in the setting of a great assize; there may be such a thing as 'the wrath of God', although we cannot reconcile the angry and sadistic God of Jonathan Edwards with the God and Father of our Lord Jesus Christ. Indeed, there *is* a hell, and there *is* a judgement, and there *is* the wrath of God. We do not even need to project our thought into another world to know the reality behind these conceptions. By their folly and sin people make hell for themselves and others in this world, and why should they not take it with them into the next? What need is there of agony of body when the mind of itself can create such torment? Judgement, too, begins here and now. In his play, *Outward*

* See R. H. Thouless: *An Introduction to the Psychology of Religion*, pp. 153 f.

Bound, Sutton Vane describes the thoughts and feelings of people who are dead though they do not know it, on the mysterious ship which they presently discover is carrying them into the other world. The siren sounds and the vessel stops.

Duke. We can none of us get away. We've stopped for good now. This is the judgement.

Tom (*pulling himself together*). No, it can't be. Here in the smoke-room of a liner?

Duke. Why shouldn't it be in the smoke-room of a liner? Have any of us really ever troubled very much to think where-and-how-and-when it might be?

Yes, why shouldn't it be in the smoke-room of a liner? It *is* in the place where we happen to be—in factory or office, shop or study, street or home. In a special sense the *crisis* of death is judgement, since we are stripped of all the defences behind which we have sheltered on earth—wealth, position, drink or whatever it may be. Nor can 'the wrath of God' be dismissed as an outworn phrase to be banished from enlightened modern minds. Dr C. H. Dodd thinks that by 'the wrath of God' (*Romans* i.18) Paul did not mean a feeling of anger on the part of God, or an attitude of God to man, but that he retained the phrase 'to describe an inevitable process of cause and effect in a moral universe'.* We live in a world where certain moral laws operate inevitably. 'Be not deceived; God is not mocked: for whatsoever a man soweth, that shall he also reap' (*Galatians* vi. 7). He shall, and there is no escape. We cannot believe, as some Old Testament writers did, that wrong-doing will in the end certainly bring disease or disaster. That view does not stand up to our observation of life. We *can* believe that evil within us, even if it does not find expression in action, leads to deterioration in character and quality. That *does* stand up to our observation, and to our own bitter experience. We should not be dealing faithfully with souls for whom we are responsible to God if we did not warn them plainly of these perils. The preacher, as we shall say in another

* *The Moffatt Commentary, Romans*, p. 23.

chapter, should not increase the *anxiety* to which some in his congregation are already too prone, for anxiety is irrational or disproportionate fear. But he should not conceal a real peril when it threatens immortal souls. He should expose its true nature so that it may be seen and feared for what it is. The man who feels fear in the presence of danger is neither neurotic nor cowardly. He is a normal human being. Anyone who 'doesn't know what fear is' must be completely lacking in sensitivity and imagination. As preachers we must try to allay anxiety, but we must awaken fear, not by lurid pictures which arouse morbid emotions, but by a plain presentation of actual perils.

There are, however, narrow limits to what can be achieved by an appeal to fear. A man may be restrained from doing evil by fear of displeasing God or setting in motion a process which will end in disaster. He may even be constrained to perform some of his duties to God and man. But fear is not a truly creative power in human personality; it stimulates self-regarding motives and leads to contraction rather than expansion. It does not enable people to enter freely and gladly into the lives of others, and while it may produce a correct and formal righteousness, which is hard and unattractive, it does not create the spontaneous goodness which is the expression of the Christian spirit.

To all this, and much more, love, not fear, is the key. But the preacher must give thought to the meaning of 'love' in this connection. There is no room here for sentimental conceptions. Nor in order to make God 'lovable' must His stature be so reduced that He is no greater than a next-door neighbour who can be clapped on the back and called by his first name. If we are to use the word 'love' to describe man's proper attitude to God, then it must ever be a love which is mindful of a majesty beyond our comprehension and a holiness which no man can bear to look upon.

Dr Moffatt points out that Jesus says little about love for God. In His teaching, as recorded in the Synoptic Gospels, the normal attitude of man to God is faith rather than love. 'The reason for this is not that Jesus could assume love for God as an inherited religious principle in the experience of His disciples, but that He preferred "faith" as a deeper expression of man's relationship to God. Trust in the divine love and power was evidently a more adequate term than love, in His mind. And reflection justifies this. For we cannot speak of loving God in precisely the same sense as we speak of loving one another; the former "love" includes nothing of the chivalrous and protecting attitude, nothing of the pardoning element, which enters into human love between human beings. Love to others includes the motive of enriching and developing their lives, also, and this is absent from the thought of love to God. Besides, "love" does not necessarily emphasise the humble trust which, for Jesus, was so vital in man's relationship to God. . . . For Jesus faith means humble insight into the reality of God, which reality is "love"—in the sense of a gracious, wise purpose, neither sentimental nor indulgent but morally strong, with a kind, stern control, which meets men in the discipline and duties of life. Reverent trust in the good-will of God as the royal Father becomes, therefore, the natural expression for man's attitude to Him.'*

The Gospel is good news of a God who cares for men so much that He takes the initiative in seeking and saving them. He was 'in Christ reconciling the world unto Himself', and the Cross is the measure of His love. Preachers who hold a penal or sub-stitutionary doctrine of the Atonement do not find it difficult to move men by persuading them that Christ bore their punish-ment or provided a sacrifice which paid their debt and set them free. But those who preach a 'subjective' or 'moral influence' interpretation are not bereft of an appeal to deep emotion if they show how Christ went to the Cross giving everything, that He might reveal the love of God in such a way that a response of trustful love might be awakened in the hard hearts of men.

(c) *The appeal to conscience.* It is said that Lacordaire, the famous French Dominican preacher of the nineteenth century, once visited

---

* *Love in the New Testament,* pp. 94–5.

a village and listened to the preaching of the local priest—a saintly soul with a wonderful pastoral gift but no talent for oratory. The villagers expressed their astonishment that so great a man should deign to listen to one who was so inferior to himself as a speaker. But Lacordaire replied, 'When I preach people crowd the churches, and even sit on the top of the confession boxes to hear me; but when your saintly priest preaches they go into the confessionals.' It may be that, after all, the obscure priest was the better preacher, for he knew how to touch the conscience.

We shall leave any discussion of the nature of conscience, and of the problem presented to the preacher by the oversensitive or morbid conscience, until a later chapter. Here we will only consider briefly how we are to reach the rather tough and impenitent consciences of the majority of our hearers.

It is not to be done primarily by denunciation. Except in the case of the already hypersensitive conscience, excessive denunciation, like nagging, is likely to produce a reaction of obstinacy. Moreover, there are people who will tell a preacher that they like plain speaking, and they hope he will give it to them 'straight from the shoulder'. But he knows that there will be no repentance or amendment of life. Some even enjoy a verbal scourging. Speaking at a conference I once called such people 'moral masochists', and being asked afterwards what the words meant, I tried to explain it in a rhyme. It appeared subsequently in *The Congregational Quarterly*, and as it is the only 'poem' of mine that has ever been published or is ever likely to be, I take leave to quote it now:

> Before the Reformation
> To escape from vile temptation
> People commonly became a monk or nun.
> In these rigid dispensations.
> They found some compensations,
> But they certainly eschewed a lot of fun.

To suppress their sinful urges
They flayed their backs with scourges,
   Or pummelled one another with their fists.
And, as they did their whacking,
Said, 'We do enjoy a smacking!'
   Now these, my little man, were masochists.

In this enlightened generation
We dislike such flagellation.
   'These people need', we say, 'psychiatrists.'
But if you're made to squirm,
And say, 'How nice to feel a worm!'
   You are, my child, a moral masochist.

For when a preacher lashes
And scars your soul with gashes,
   You feel a strange elation down inside.
If you're properly remorseful,
There's no need to be resourceful,
   The verbal flagellation saves your pride!

The sense of sin may be aroused in two ways. First, it may follow from the realisation that something good, to which one should have responded, has been rejected. Therefore, the preacher needs less to denounce evil than to present a compelling picture of goodness. In other words, he has to present Christ. Bishop Linton, who was an outstandingly successful missionary in Persia, said that the sense of sin was produced not by denunciation but by the vision of Christ's perfect manhood.

Dear Master, in whose life I see
All that I would, but fail to be,
Let Thy clear light for ever shine,
To shame and guide this life of mine.

Though what I dream and what I do
In my weak days are always two,
Help me, oppressed by things undone,
O Thou, whose deeds and dreams were one.
                                        JOHN HUNTER

Secondly, conscience is touched by the realisation of the con-
sequences in the lives of others of what we are or what we have
done. One of the results of sin is a loss of spiritual sensitivity, so
that we cannot see the effect it is having within ourselves. It has
been said that sin is unlike all other things, in that the more you
practise it the less you know of its real nature. But sometimes
the awareness of what our sins are doing in the lives of others
pulls us up with a shock. This happened to John de Stogumber,
the English chaplain in Shaw's *St. Joan*. He was fanatical in his
efforts to have the Maid burned at the stake, and he went out to
watch the end and gloat over his triumph. But in the light of the
flames he saw his own sin for the first time. The revelation was
too much for him, and filled with sudden remorse he rushed
away from the sight he could not stand and cried to Warwick, 'My
lord, my lord: for Christ's sake, pray for my wretched guilty
soul. . . . I meant no harm. I did not know what it would be like.
. . . I let them do it. If I had known, I would have torn her from
their hands.'
    But it is at the Cross of Christ that a man receives the most
devastating self-revelation. The preacher must show that He
who, alone of all men, was perfectly good and utterly loving,
was brought to that horror of spiritual and physical agony by
sin—not by sins possible only to monsters of iniquity and in-
conceivable by decent men, but by ordinary sins of ordinary
people. Let the preacher sometimes work out in detail the sins
which caused the crucifixion—pride, jealousy, greed, indifference, cowardice—and every soul in the congregation will say,
'I was there when they crucified my Lord.'
    Of course, there will always be people in the congregation

who will raise every possible defence to shield themselves from the impact of truth upon their consciences. These defences the preacher must recognise, and learn how to penetrate them. I have called one of them 'moral masochism'. There are many others, and we shall consider some of them when we come later to the preaching of Christian ethics.*

* See note on p, 106.

CHAPTER FIVE

Pastoral Preaching

Some years ago a medical psychologist was talking to me about his work. Like most of his profession he was an overworked man. His main job was the superintending of a great mental institution with some two thousand resident patients, but, as is the way with such men, he did all sorts of other things to fill in his spare time! He was then running psychological clinics at a couple of hospitals which he visited once a week. The whole thing, he said, was profoundly unsatisfactory. How could he give the patients who crowded his clinics the help they needed? Nobody knew better than he that some of them ought to have an hour to themselves every time he saw them, and yet he had to deal with a whole lot of patients in the course of a single afternoon. Then he said abruptly, 'Most of these patients should never have come to me; they should have gone to you'. He was, of course, speaking to me as the representative of my profession. He meant that if they had in the first place taken their troubles to a minister equipped with some understanding of human nature and gifted with sympathy, some of them would never have become mentally, and perhaps physically, ill. They would not have generated within themselves pent-up anxiety which, in the end, could be released only by the prolonged efforts of a specialist. Although he was too kind to say it in so many words, the doctor was really telling us parsons that we are not doing our job; we are neglecting one side of it pretty badly. So far as it is being done at all, we are putting an unfair share of it on the shoulders of overworked people like himself, whose highly trained skill and specialised knowledge should be kept for those who are so

94

seriously ill that no one less qualified can help them. Was the doctor right in his implied accusation?

When I have been asked to talk to groups of ministers and clergy about pastoral work, I have sometimes been amazed to hear men, who have been in the ministry for years, saying that it is the rarest thing in the world for anybody to consult them about moral and emotional troubles. People come to them when forms have to be signed or Johnny has to be found a job, but they never come to talk about their real troubles. They do not bring to the minister their tangled personal relationships, their fears and anxieties, their temptations and burden of guilt, their resentments and frustrations.

If people do not come to him with their personal problems, the first question a minister should ask himself is: What is wrong with my preaching? In the ordinary course of his ministry a man will deal with an enormous variety of subjects and will preach many different types of sermons. Some will have little immediate bearing on the personal problems of the individuals who make up his congregation, but he will not be doing his work as a preacher unless, after most of his sermons, somebody says to himself, 'Here is a man interested in human problems, who seems to know what goes on in people's minds. He might be able to help *me*.' If he is really on the spot, some of his hearers will often say, 'He can't really know about me, but he might have preached that sermon specially for me.' There are always in a congregation people who are longing to talk over their difficulties with someone who will be understanding and helpful. (I don't mean people who *will* talk about themselves to everybody they meet—and nothing can stop them!) There are others who have shut themselves up with their troubles and do not want to talk about them to anybody, although they, of all people, most need that relief. Sometimes a preacher penetrates even these defensive walls of reserve, so that one of his hearers almost rushes to his vestry and blurts out, 'I didn't think I should ever breathe a word of this to a living soul, but . . .', and out it all comes.

So it may well be that, when you preach, there is somebody in the congregation, someone in desperate need, who is asking himself, 'I wonder if I could go and talk to him? Would he have patience to listen to me? And would he understand?' He is trying to sum you up, and probably he is doing it pretty accurately. 'There is nothing', says Jung, 'finer than a neurotic's intuition.'* Many people in the pews are 'neurotic'. If it comes to that we all are, more or less, in pew and pulpit alike. I am not, of course, using the word in the wrong and disparaging sense that is often given to it in common speech. I mean that many people in every congregation are suffering from 'nerves', from anxieties and emotional tangles which unfit them for living with other people or make life a hell for them, and which possibly cause them to make a hell for others.

If a person with troubles of this sort decides to seek help, it will probably be because the preacher has won his confidence by the way he preaches, the things he says, and, most of all, by the revelation of his personality. And, remember, it is in many cases no easy decision to make. It means dragging out into the light things that have been kept hidden for years because they seemed too painful or too shameful to talk about. And there is something irretrievable about the business. A secret once out cannot be recalled. Especially if the 'patient' is a member of your own congregation and not a stranger whose path need never cross yours again unless he chooses; he may find it an ordeal to undress his mind and soul in your presence. He may fear that he will always feel naked and ashamed when he meets you about the church premises or on social occasions.

What, then, must the preacher convey to the troubled soul in his congregation?

(1) *That he is approachable*

For many people the very fact that a man is a minister constitutes a barrier that has to be broken through. If, in addition, he is

* C. Jung: *Analytical Psychology*, 2nd ed., p. 262.

pompous or cold, remote or dreamy, the barrier may be impassable. Eric Gill says in his autobiography that he never met a parson with whom he could talk as man to man. Most people feel like that about parsons and always keep up some sort of pose in their presence. But the troubled fellow in your congregation must be able to feel that he can drop all disguises and talk to you simply as one human being to another. It will help him to feel like that if, in your sermon, you have already talked to him as man to man. And here we must recall what has already been said earlier about extempore preaching and freedom to look the congregation in the eyes. It may be that an academic kind of sermon or one compact of theological argument does not lose a great deal by being read or delivered from closely followed notes—though even that I find hard to believe. That a pastoral sermon loses almost everything I am quite certain. You cannot *read* to a man a dissertation about the things that are tearing his life apart! You cannot get home to him if your eyes are down on the reading desk or up in the rafters. You must talk to him and you must look at him. You must not, of course, stare or glare at him, or you will frighten him away, but your eyes must make contact with him, bridging the distance and creating an intimacy of relationship. In other words, by talking to him you must help him to feel what it would be like to talk to you across the hearth, and see to it that he does not find the prospect too forbidding.

(2) *That he is human*

I once heard it proclaimed from a barber's chair by an ex-mayor of the town where I then lived, that all parsons are, in secret, hard drinkers and licentious livers. 'Damned lot of hypocrites!', he said. He had not noticed that I was sitting in the next chair but one and was taken aback when, at the conclusion of operations, I went over to him. At once he became almost abject in his apologies. 'I am sorry, sir,' he said. 'I had no idea you were here. I should not have used bad language in your presence.' I told him I was not in the least troubled about his 'bad language', which was merely silly anyway, but that it would be a good thing if he would have some regard for the truth. There are a lot of people whose opinion of parsons is pretty much like his. They are not very likely to be found in church. Indeed, their professed contempt for parsons is a well-worn excuse for staying away.

There may, however, be someone in the congregation who holds a very different, but equally unrealistic, view of ministers. He supposes that the man in the pulpit is not like other men, that he lives in a rarefied spiritual atmosphere. If he has any temptations at all, which is hardly to be imagined, they must be such very refined ones that they are incomprehensible to the likes of him. And equally his temptations would not be comprehensible to a being so far removed from common earth. 'Suppose I did go and unburden myself to the preacher, would he condemn me, would he be shocked, or would he just not understand what I was talking about?'

A 'pastoral' sermon is badly wide of the mark unless it convinces the man in the pew that the preacher is human like himself, and that he will neither condemn nor recoil, but seek to understand. He must be sure that the preacher has sympathy, which is neither pity nor sentimentality, but the power of thinking and living yourself into the lives of other people. It means the ability to realise what the other fellow actually feels, and not what you think he ought to feel, or what you suppose you would feel if you were in his place, for his temperament, upbringing and experience are different from yours. The anxious and troubled person is always inwardly lonely, and, as Halliday says, one of the main purposes of sympathy is the destruction of solitude,* and the giving of encouragement and strength in the midst of difficulty. Jung describes the physician as the 'companion of the soul'. The man who is lonely, and helplessly inadequate in his loneliness, needs a companion of the soul, and hopes, as he has every right to hope, that he will find one in the preacher. You, as a preacher, must make him feel that he is not seeking in vain, that

* Halliday: *Psychology and Religious Experience,* p. 121.

you will let him lean for a time upon your strength, or rather, upon the strength of God mediated through you, in order that presently he may stand upon his own feet. He must not sense in you a sentimental kind of pity which would weaken him by letting him lean for ever, but the kind of strong, effective sympathy which would enter into his situation in order to help him to transform defeat into victory.

(3) *That he knows his job*

Jung reminds us that it is the priest or minister, rather than the doctor, who should be most concerned with the problem of spiritual suffering. In most cases the sufferer consults the doctor first because he supposes himself to be physically ill. 'There are, however, persons who, while well aware of the psychic nature of their complaint, nevertheless refuse to turn to the clergyman. They do not believe that he can really help them. Such persons distrust the doctor for the same reason, and they are justified by the fact that both doctor and clergyman stand before them with empty hands, if not what is worse—with empty words. We can hardly expect the doctor to have anything to say about the ultimate questions of the soul. It is from the clergyman, not from the doctor, that the sufferer should expect such help.' Jung points out that Protestants are much more ready than Catholics to assume, and with good reason, that the minister of their church will be without adequate psychological knowledge. He carried out an investigation which showed that 57 per cent. of the Protestants would go to a doctor and only 25 per cent. of the Catholics, while only 8 per cent. of the Protestants would go to a minister as against 58 per cent. of the Catholics. As their reason for not consulting the minister 52 per cent. gave his lack of psychological knowledge.*

That is a terrible indictment. We cannot deny the truth of it, though we may hope that the situation is improving. The minister is not called to be a specialist in psycho-therapy, but he ought

* C. Jung: *Modern Man in Search of a Soul*, p. 262.

to have enough psychological knowledge to enable him to help the comparatively simple kind of case that is properly within his province. If he has not got it, it is pious fraud on his part to pretend that he has. If he does possess it, his preaching should convey the impression that he knows a great deal about people, about their emotional difficulties and the strange tricks their minds can play.

But he must not say that he does! Advertising should be banned in the pulpit as well as on the B.B.C.! Nor should he try to present his credentials by retailing the 'cases' that he has handled successfully after the manner of the testimonials beloved by the advertisers of patent medicines. Those tactics can be so employed in the pulpit that one feels the preacher will inevitably add, 'The originals can be seen on application at the vestry.' A minister who quotes cases in that way will, in fact, prevent the establishment of the confidence he is striving after. The anxious soul in the pew will probably decide on the spot that he is not going to risk providing next Sunday's extract from the case-book. No more effective will be the use of psychological jargon. It will be suspected at once that the preacher is trying to create an impression. A few of the ignorant may be duly impressed, but the more intelligent will reflect that one who has mastered his subject can generally express himself in terms 'understanded of the people'. The man who is a good pastoral preacher speaks of human needs and difficulties in a simple, direct and sympathetic way, so that some of his hearers say, 'He knows what goes on in people's lives. I believe he can help *me*.'

Yes, perhaps he can. But the help that even the most effective preacher can give in a sermon is limited.

In the first place, it is clear that a sermon can deal with personal problems only in a general way. The doctor who frequently speaks on the wireless in the mornings sometimes describes diseases, suggests possible causes or talks about methods of cure. Further than that he will not, and cannot, go. He does not say, 'If you think you have the disease I've been talking about, give yourself a dozen injections of this or that.' He says, 'Go and see your own doctor.' The reason is, of course, that a doctor, at any rate a good one, does not treat diseases; he treats patients. He has to discover the cause of the trouble, which may differ from one case to another, and in treatment he will often take into consideration the physical constitution, the temperament and personality of the patient. But the role of the wireless doctor is not without value. He has probably helped many people to begin to understand their own condition; he has given some a hope that they can be cured; and he has persuaded many to take steps to deal with their trouble before it has reached the chronic or incurable stage.

There are doubtless listeners who think that the doctor should be able to give them over the wireless some advice or prescription which would meet their need even though he has never seen them. And those who have had experience of giving talks on personal problems or pastoral psychology will be familiar enough with the person who gets up during question-time, describes his own or somebody else's symptoms in about thirty seconds, and expects to be told the diagnosis and cure on the spot. Of course, it can't be done. In any congregation there will be many cases of anxiety. No, that is not the right way to put it. There will be many *anxious people*. No two of them will be alike, and their anxiety will arise from many different causes. Every one, like the doctor's patients, will have to be treated as an individual.

> There is no expeditious road
> To pack and label men for God,
> And save them by the barrel-load.

And there is no expeditious road to deal with the bewildering variety of personal problems and relieve anxiety by the barrel-load!

The function of the preacher, then, is, in this matter, rather like that of the wireless doctor. He speaks to a large number of people in general terms. He does not cure them by public speech, but he hopes to create the conditions in which the real work of cure can begin. Whether or not a doctor speaking on the wireless is essential to the health of the nation, this function of the preacher is necessary to the mental and spiritual health of a congregation.

Secondly, preaching is not enough because the wrong person is doing all the talking! An individual full of anxiety, resentments and emotional tangles is not going to be 'cured' by being talked to for a solid half-hour without interruption. In the end it is not what is said to him but what he says which will relieve his inner tensions. That is a point which preachers should take to heart, because some of us still want to do all the talking in the vestry as well as in the pulpit. It is not what *we* see, and tell the 'patient' that we see, which will enable him to re-adjust himself to life, but what he comes to see with a little gentle and unobtrusive guidance from us, as he 'gets things off his chest' and liberates his pent-up and repressed emotions.

So much, then, for what pastoral preaching cannot do—it cannot be made a substitute for personal dealing or 'counselling'. But there is much that it can do.

(a) *Preaching can prepare the way for personal dealing.* No minister has any right to preach pastoral sermons unless he is prepared for the personal interviews which may arise from them. Dr H. J. S. Guntrip tells of a young man who did 'screw up his courage to go to the vestry after service and lay a very big problem before a very famous preacher. In his own words, "The great man was obviously anxious to get home to his supper and cut short my halting statement with a few encouraging platitudes and the assurance that 'things would turn out all right'. I left feeling let down and in despair. I could not talk of my problem at home, and knew no one else who seemed likely to understand." '* However much 'the great man' wanted his supper, he should at least have shown a sympathetic attitude, and if hunger or any other reason

* H. J. S. Guntrip: *Mental Pain and the Cure of Souls,* pp. 17 f.

had made that hour and place inopportune, he should have arranged a time when he could have devoted himself to listening and helping. If the need was urgent or if it was likely that the youth would not bring his courage to the sticking-point again, only something much more serious than an appetite for supper could condone the failure to deal with the situation then and there. Every minister will sometimes have the bitter experience of finding himself unable to cope with the difficulties of those who seek his aid, but no one, in the name of common honesty and decency, should preach sermons which will bring needy and expectant souls to him unless he is ready to spend and be spent for their sakes, and unless he is prepared to make himself as competent as possible to give them help.

(b) *Preaching can assure people that they are not alone in their difficulties and troubles.* Many people suffer from the illusion that they are unique. They imagine that nobody else has difficulties like theirs; nobody else could be so wicked or so weak. Some time ago, in a series of broadcast talks, I explored a little the nature and causes of religious doubts. In letter after letter listeners said they had no idea that others had doubts like theirs; it had helped them just to know that they were not alone. Nobody who has seen it will forget the look of relief and gratitude which comes over a man's face when he is assured that things which he thought put him beyond the pale are common human problems, or the light which shines in his eyes when he is told that others have overcome temptations and failures like his. Until that moment he has felt himself quite alone; now he is in company. He has believed 'There is nothing I can do'; now he says: 'If they could do it, so can I.'

(c) *Preaching can help people to see the constructive possibilities in every experience.* George Eliot says, 'It would be a poor result of all our anguish and wrestling if we won nothing but our old selves at the end of it.' It would, indeed. A great deal of life would be wasted, whereas doubts may be the way to stronger faith, temptations the tensions by which the sinews of the soul are strengthened, sorrow the hard school in which sympathy is learned, and even sin the means whereby we reach a deeper understanding of the love of God and a wider and gentler charity towards our fellows. The preacher can show people how to pick up the broken fragments of life that nothing be lost. It is not only those whose lives are already broken who need to learn how to do that. 'Man is born to trouble as the sparks fly upwards', and none can hope to escape, or should desire to do so, for then he would know 'the horror of immunity'. It is well that people should learn, before the severest trials and troubles overtake them, an attitude towards all the experiences of life which will save them from bitterness and turn loss into gain.

(d) *Preaching can give the assurance of a Power available in time of need.* Some of the anxious and troubled people in the congregation have probably been told by their families or friends to 'pull yourself together' or 'snap out of it'. In some cases that advice may have been sound enough; in others it was blundering or cruel. The sufferer has replied, bitterly but truthfully, that he has tried and tried to use his will, but it will not work. For that there may be two reasons. Either some unconscious factors are rendering the will impotent, or the man has failed so often that he does not believe it is possible to succeed. The picture of failure is so firmly settled in his mind that there has come into operation what Baudouin calls 'the law of reversed effort'—when the imagination and the will are in conflict the imagination always wins. Release from this crippling feeling of impotence will come through the faith that there is a Power outside the man, and greater than himself, which is available to him in his weakness. The New Testament speaks again and again of such a power. In the Fourth Gospel Jesus promises to His disciples the gift of the 'Comforter', the indwelling Spirit who will impart strength. (The word 'Comforter' is derived from the Latin *fortis*, which means 'strong'.) The letters of Paul are full of the conviction, derived from his own experience and observation, that by His Spirit working in man God gives a power which creates love and all the other qualities of Christian character, transforms personality and makes a man able for anything. Sometimes he speaks of the Spirit of God, sometimes of the Spirit of Christ, sometimes of the Power of God, but they are all ways of describing the wonderful power which is at work in men's lives.

This doctrine of the Holy Spirit, however it is expressed, means that there is power outside of a man which he can appropriate and use. That such power is available is an idea not confined to theologians. Dr J. A. Hadfield points out that the theories of many modern psychologists suggest that 'we are not merely receptacles but *channels* of energy. Man's might is not to be measured by the stagnant water in the well, but by the limitless supply from the clouds of heaven.* That is a good enough description of the Christian faith and experience if we remember that we have to do not with an impersonal force but with a Personal Influence. The point to remember and impress upon the congregation is that the power is something which is *given*. It is not a thing to be secured by striving. It comes when we cease to strive; it surges in when we open our lives to it. Paul gives us to understand, says Dr C. H. Dodd, that 'the immense energies of the religious life are rooted in a moment of passivity in which God acts'.†

All of this the preacher will proclaim—will proclaim, we may hope, with a conviction born of experience. There will be people in his congregation who will feel the need of such a power to overcome their impotence and despair. Yet they will not be able to receive it in spite of his assurance that it is theirs for the taking. The channels are blocked, and it is unlikely that any amount of

* *The Spirit*, edited by B. H. Streeter.
† *Moffatt Commentary on Romans*, p. 16. I have tried to work out this idea of power more fully in a sermon entitled "Power for Christian Living" in *My Way of Preaching*, edited by Robert J. Smithson (Pickering & Inglis).

preaching will clear them. That will be done only by much patient work in study or vestry, when preacher and hearer together set about discovering and clearing away the obstacles— the anxiety, resentments, moral failures or intellectual difficulties —so that the power of God may flow freely in. But if the gospel of God's power answering human need had never been preached, the man would have stumbled on in impotence and despair without knowing that a new life of freedom was possible even for him. So it is worth while, after all, to be a preacher!

NOTE

Chapter Four closes with the words 'when we come later to the preaching of Christian ethics'. It is clear from these words that Mr Tizard's whole plan was never completed. We do not know how much more he had in mind to add, except that there was to be at least a chapter on the preaching of Christian ethics. His unexpected death at the early age of fifty-five years deprived the Church of an outstanding preacher and minister, at a time when he had several projects in mind for further writing. Of these, the present book was most nearly complete, though it is probable that, had he lived, there would have been more than one further chapter.

His papers have been found to contain some fifty or more pages in pencilled manuscript of a book on Middle Age. This was to be a sequel to his earlier *Guide to Marriage*. It has proved possible to utilize this manuscript, along with a certain amount of additional material, to make up a book that will preserve for us a further legacy of Mr Tizard's gathered wisdom about human living, on a subject about which he felt a special interest.

H. GUNTRIP